Thriving as a Single Person in Ministry

Thriving as a Single Person in Ministry

Kevin E. Lawson and Jane Carr

An Alban Institute Book

ROWMAN & LITTLEFIELD
Lanham • Boulder • New York • London

Published by Rowman & Littlefield

An imprint of The Rowman & Littlefield Publishing Group, Inc.
4501 Forbes Boulevard, Suite 200, Lanham, Maryland 20706
www.rowman.com
6 Tinworth Street, London SE11 5AL, United Kingdom

British Library Cataloguing in Publication Information Available

Library of Congress Cataloging-in-Publication Data on File

ISBN 978-1-5381-2750-6 (cloth: alk. paper)
ISBN 978-1-5381-2751-3 (pbk.: alk. paper)
ISBN 978-1-5381-2749-0 (ebook)

∞™ The paper used in this publication meets the minimum requirements of American National Standard for Information Sciences—Permanence of Paper for Printed Library Materials, ANSI/NISO Z39.48–1992.

Contents

Introduction

Singles in Ministry: A Growing and Welcome Presence

We are so glad you have chosen to read this book, and we hope you find much in it to either help you in your own ministry if you are single or help you better support others you know who serve on church staff while single. This is our deepest desire and hope. For more than a quarter century, we have both been involved in equipping and encouraging people in vocational ministry, seeking to prepare students well for ministry leadership roles and to support people in these roles so they can thrive in their ministries. This is definitely a calling for us, one that brings us great joy and satisfaction, and this book flows out of that sense of calling. Here's a little more about us.

Jane served on church staff for twenty-six years, with seven of these years as a single adult in her twenties, and nineteen more following her marriage to Gary at age twenty-nine. Her early years of ministry included oversight of children, student, and singles ministries, leading thirty-two paid staff members and thousands of volunteers. In her later years of ministry, she provided oversight to employee hiring, performance management, and development of over seventy paid employees, and the launch of a comprehensive internship program. She has taught in both undergraduate and graduate Christian ministry programs for over twenty years and maintains contacts with many alumni. Jane has helped raise up a generation of church ministry leaders and is a mentor and role model to many former staff members, students, and graduates—especially young women in ministry. In addition to her work in the church and academia, she is the principal owner of Focus on Leaders, a business she launched in 2014 to provide executive coaching and leadership development programs to churches and corporate leaders.

Kevin served on church staff for eleven years. In all of these years, he was married to his wife, Patty, who was a great support in the midst of ministry challenges. They recently celebrated their forty-first wedding anniversary. He has taught in undergraduate and graduate programs in Christian ministry for almost thirty years. In addition, he has pursued research and writing on what helps people to thrive in associate staff ministry[1] and how ministry supervisors can help their staff to thrive. Some of this research he carried out with his friend and colleague, Mick Boersma,[2] whose big heart of love and compassion for church staff members has no equal.

This earlier research and writing has been well received, and some readers have sent us words of appreciation. In recent years we have also received requests to write more about the ministry experience of a growing population—those who are single on church staff—and what they can do to thrive in their ministry roles. These kinds of requests are what led Jane and I to pursue our research, to listen to what our single church staff colleagues have to say, and to write this book.[3]

CHANGING ADULT DEMOGRAPHICS AND THE CHURCH

To start with, let's review what is happening in our society regarding marriage and singleness. It is clear that marital status patterns have been changing in Western society, in general, and the United States, in particular. More people are spending a significant amount of their adult lives single, including many who never marry, and it is impacting what we see in our communities, our congregations, and on our church staffs. Here is some of what we have seen changing over the past few decades:

- More people are delaying marriage until later in their adult lives. In 1970, the average age of first marriage in the United States was twenty-one for women and twenty-three for men. Almost fifty years later, these ages have shifted upward to twenty-eight for women and thirty for men.[4]
- An increasing number of adults are currently single. The U.S. census data in 2016 revealed that 45 percent of Americans, ages eighteen and over, were single. Of these, 64 percent had never been married, 23 percent were divorced, and 13 percent were widowed.[5] Some other data sources have claimed that over 50 percent of American adults are currently single, but these may not be as accurate as the census data.
- The number of single person households has also grown. In early 2018, CNN reported that 42 percent of adults were living in single person households, up from 39 percent in 2007.[6]

In light of these changes in our culture, with marriage being increasingly delayed and more people seeking divorces, it is clear that the number of single adults within our churches has also grown. Whatever the exact current percentage, this increasing number of single adults within our churches needs our best prayerful reflection on how to serve them well and help them to grow in their discipleship with Christ. While not the focus of this book, this is an issue that forms a backdrop for our main focus on challenges for single church staff members.

THE GROWING NUMBER OF SINGLE CHURCH STAFF MEMBERS

As more young adults delay marriage, date longer before becoming married, or stay single, it is clear that we are also seeing an increase in the number of church staff members who are single, particularly in associate staff roles (e.g., children's ministry, youth ministry, and young adult ministry). While for younger staff members, who more commonly serve in associate staff ministry roles, this may change as time goes by and many eventually marry, it seems that an increasing number of others will continue to be single throughout their ministry service. This represents a bit of a cultural change on church staffs that needs to be recognized. Historically, in the Protestant movement, most church staff members, particularly ordained clergy, have been married, but this is changing. Single staff members must learn how to navigate ministry challenges that can come from serving in churches with a high value on family and on "family ministry," and supervisors have to rethink what to expect from staff members who are single and how to best supervise and support them as they serve. While many of their needs are the same as married staff members, some needs, and much of their experience of being a church staff member, are different.

THE NEED FOR A THEOLOGY OF SINGLENESS IN MINISTRY: LEARNING FROM JESUS AND PAUL

One final observation before we review the structure and flow of this book: an irony several of the single church staff members we interviewed pointed out was how often people in their church leadership teams, if asked, would acknowledge that (1) Jesus was single, (2) the Apostle Paul was single, and (3) 1 Corinthians 7 affirms the value of living as a single person—and yet, these same church leaders still preferred that staff members in the church, particularly if they are male, be married. One shared that leaders in his church acknowledged that their insistence on pastoral staff being married was not biblical, yet it was still required. For single women in ministry, there is a clearly felt expectation that they will eventually marry and that being single in ministry is definitely not normal. In light of the growing trend of delayed marriage and the gifting and calling of single people of all ages, both men and women, to minister within the church, it is high time that denominational and congregational leaders work through their theology of ministry leadership and consider more carefully the role of singles in ministry.

What can we learn from a closer examination of the lives and ministry of Jesus, Paul, and other disciples who may have been single? How do we respond today to Paul's instruction to the Corinthian church that it is good for people to remain single if they can (1 Corinthians 7:8, 26) and that those who marry will have worldly troubles and be anxious about worldly things that lead to divided interests (vv. 28, 33)? What other passages of Scripture need our careful study to help us build a stronger theology of both singleness and marriage? What might also help those who are "in between"—in committed relationships but not yet in a position to marry? Who might they learn from in Scripture and what guidance is there for them and the church for how to include them well?

While the development of a theology of singleness in general[7] or of singleness in ministry leadership is not the purpose of this book, we do believe there are a few teachings from Scripture that are foundational to consider and build upon. We offer these to stimulate all of our thinking and urge church and denominational leaders to study this issue more fully, listen carefully to singles within their midst, and allow their study findings and growing understanding of singles' experiences in the church to help develop faithful ministry practice. Here are seven foundational truths that we believe Scripture affirms that can move us forward in the development of a theology of singleness:[8]

1. While marriage is a "good thing" that God blesses and uses for many people's growth, and as a context for raising and nurturing children, it is clear that marriage is not everyone's calling. Genesis 1 and 2 affirm aspects of this in the creation account. There are many examples in Scripture of faithful people who are single (e.g., Anna in Luke 2, Timothy, Paul). A passage in 1 Corinthians 7 is the key that warrants careful study on several of these points, including this first one.
2. Living as a single person is a normal experience. For some, this will be for short seasons of life (e.g., before marriage, as a widow or widower, following a divorce). For others, this will be their long-term life experience. While this can have its challenges and may not be what all are called to pursue, it also has its opportunities for other enriching relationships and ministry opportunities. People are not "incomplete" while single, waiting for completion in marriage, but whole persons who are able to be in loving relationships with others. Again, 1 Corinthians 7 is a key passage for exploring these issues.

3. Adult discipleship and growth in maturity in our walk with Christ is enhanced by many different kinds of relationships and mutual ministry (see 1 Peter 4:10–11), and marriage is not a requirement for reaching emotional or spiritual maturity. All people have areas where growth is needed, and this can happen through relationships at work, in the church, and in families. The household codes in Ephesians 5–6 and Colossians 3–4 are examples of how different relationships can become "laboratories"—opportunities for growth in love and righteousness. Ephesians 4:11–16 makes it clear that it is within the context of the church, as we all contribute to the building up of the Body of Christ, that our growth in Christlikeness occurs. While God certainly uses marriage relationships for our growth, the primary context for growth toward maturity in Christ is within the church.
4. God gifts and calls people to serve God's people as members of the Body of Christ, including people of all ages, genders, races, and marital statuses. Both 1 Corinthians 12 and Ephesians 4 emphasize how God gifts the various members of the church in ways to contribute to its growth. Those who are single have much to contribute to the ministry of the church, and in some ways may be able to give more focus to their ministry (again, see 1 Corinthians 7).
5. Singleness in ministry is modeled by Jesus and both encouraged and modeled by Paul and needs to be seen as an accepted and valued status in ministry today. In his incarnation, Jesus, as fully human and fully Divine, in some ways embodies the normalcy of being single both in this earthly life and in the life to come. In his incarnation he shows us that being married was not a prerequisite for wholeness or for serving in ministry leadership, and he taught that marriage relationships are temporary, superseded by a different kind of union with God in heaven (Matthew 22: 23–33). Jesus is our prototypical human example of relationship with God. Our fundamental identity is not found in marriage on earth but in a "marriage covenant" kind of relationship with God. Paul, in a different way, is also an example of a single ministry leader, and in 1 Corinthians 7 he encourages others who are single to remain single for the sake of their ministries.
6. A call to ministry leadership does not require marriage in order to live out that call. This is clearly shown in the examples of Jesus and Paul. It may also be that some of the church leaders that Paul appointed were also single (e.g., Timothy, possibly Titus). In 1 Timothy 3:1–7 and Titus 1:5–9, while the criteria for potential "overseers" includes being "the husband of one wife," that seems to be a guard against leaders modeling polygamy in the church, not as ruling out those who are single. Timothy's leadership was commended by Paul, even though he was young, and apparently not married. This warrants further study in light of both the teaching of these letters and the examples of Jesus and Paul.

7. Finally, within Scripture, the marriage relationship is used as an image or a sign of our relationship with God (i.e., Bride of Christ), but the primary images of our relationships with one another in the church are other family ones—"brother and sister." Isaiah (54:5), Jeremiah (3:14, 31:32), and Hosea use marriage imagery for how the people of God relate to God. Ephesians 5:25–32 and Revelations 19 and 21 use "bride" imagery regarding how the church corporately relates to God as Christ's bride. But within the church, as we consider our relationships with one another, brother and sister language for followers of Christ is scattered through the New Testament. It is a dominant image used in the book of Acts (see 6:3; 11:29; 12:17; 16:40; 18:18, 27; 21:7, 17; 28:14–15). It is also used repeatedly in Romans (see 1:13; 7:1, 4; 8:12, 29; 10:1; 11:25; 12:1; 14:10–12; 15:14, 30; 16:14, 17) and is a dominant image in Paul's other letters to the churches.[9] Other references to concepts of adoption and inheritance or our position as heirs in Christ also emphasize the priority of a family understanding of our relationship as fellow believers. Our singleness or "marriedness" is less crucial for our relationship together under God than is our adoption into God's family and identity as the children of God. Contemporary emphasis on nuclear family ministry can inadvertently marginalize those who are single, while intergenerational ministry models can open opportunities for more mutual ministry and family-like support.

While not an exhaustive study by any means, together, these foundational understandings point us to the need for developing a more inclusive and supportive church environment for those who are single, and recognizing how God gifts both married and single adults for mutual ministry in the church as equal brothers and sisters in the family of God.

In addition to developing a stronger, clearer theology of singleness and ministry, it would also be helpful to look more closely at church practice over the past 2,000 years. What important considerations can we learn from the history of the church as we determine our practices today? What examples from the past highlight the opportunities and challenges of ministry while married and while single? How might this inform our practices for the supervision and support of both married and single church staff today? This is an area where much more work is needed, for the sake of the church and for all who serve within it.

THE FLOW OF THIS BOOK

This book is built around three basic questions. The first and most foundational: "What is it like to serve in vocational ministry while single?" This area has had very little attention in research with people in ministry. What we have had to date is primarily first-person stories in blogs, articles, and book chapters, with each single staff member sharing a few aspects of their own experience. In our effort to answer this foundational question, we focused on two specific aspects that reflect our two other questions: (1) "What are the opportunities and joys of ministry as a single person?" and (2) "What are the challenges of ministry as a single person, and what helps in managing these challenges?"

The structure and flow of the book reflects our efforts to answer these questions. Chapter 1 addresses the opportunities and joys those who are single find in their ministry that are enhanced in some way by their singleness. What follows are seven chapters about the main challenges of ministry when single, and what helps in navigating them well. Chapter 2 explores the experience of being single in a "family church" setting. Chapter 3 looks at the challenges of dating as a church staff member. Chapter 4 considers the financial challenges that single church staff experience. Chapter 5 looks at the challenges single people face in applying for ministry leadership roles and in how people respond to them in their ministry assignments. Chapter 6 considers single staff members' experience of loneliness in their work and the development of supportive relationships. Chapter 7 reviews the challenges single staff may face in their work relationships and explores ways to grow healthy staff relationships. Chapter 8 discusses the increased challenge of burnout that single staff members may experience, and how to promote better self-care when single.

Following the main chapters of the book, we have provided three appendices we hope will be helpful, as well. Appendix 1 is an open letter to church leaders and ministry supervisors on what they can do to better support their single church staff members. These leaders are often the ones in the best position to help address some of the more challenging aspects of the staff members' ministry experience. You can copy and share this appendix with anyone who can benefit from it. Appendix 2 is a listing of resources about and for singles who serve in ministry leadership roles. It includes all of the book chapters, articles, and blogs we found in our research. For those who want to read more on these issues, this is a place to start. Finally, Appendix 3 gives a more detailed overview of how we conducted this study and analyzed the data.

HOW TO GET THE MOST OUT OF READING THIS BOOK

For those who serve, or plan to serve on a church staff while single, we would recommend that you read through this book slowly, taking time after reading each chapter to do two things.

First, we have provided some reflection and discussion questions to help you think through your own experience in ministry and consider which of the issues within the chapter are most relevant for you. We encourage you to take time to consider these well, either on your own or with a friend or mentor, to see what might help in addressing the identified issues. Don't hurry this process, but take time to work through these issues in light of your past experience and current situation.

Second, each chapter identifies some possible issues to discuss with your ministry supervisor. Take time to consider which ones are most relevant for you and may be most profitable to talk over with your supervisor. Think about how to approach this, and see if these kinds of conversations would be good opportunities to surface and address important issues that impact your ability to thrive in ministry.

If you are a ministry supervisor and you oversee any single staff members, thank you for taking time to read this book so you can better understand their needs and how to supervise and support them well. The lists of possible issues for discussion between the ministry supervisor and the staff member would be a good place to focus your attention as you think about what you might do to help them thrive in their ministries. Take time to review these questions with them, and ask which ones would be most helpful to focus on and talk through together. It is important to ask questions and listen well to what they have to say. While there are some similarities in single church staff members' experiences, no two people and no two situations are the same. Do your best to understand their experience and perspective, and see what might be most helpful to address to support them in their service.

May God give you grace, wisdom, and perseverance to serve well where you are, and may you find joy and satisfaction in the serving.

Kevin E. Lawson and Jane Carr

Chapter 1

Maximizing Opportunities of Ministry when Single

Use the freedom you have with your schedule to, in a healthy way. Invest in others and be involved in ministry.

Take short-term mission trips or fun trips around the world.

There is so much to be seen, when you get married that will change.

Take the perks of being single and dive into them until you meet someone.

The vast majority of singles want to be married and even some day expect to be married. Several interviewees even acknowledged that at times it is challenging to see the opportunities of singleness amid societal pressures and various other challenges they face. Perspective and an appreciation for the present were important themes as our interviewees began talking about the joys and opportunities of singleness. We all know how easy it is to focus on what we don't have and in so doing miss out on what we do have. As singles reflected on the joys and opportunities of their singleness, they echoed that sentiment in phrases such as these:

> I'm not hiding, I'm not trying to be single. I have always wanted to be married and in ministry. I wanted to partner with my husband in ministry, but I have come to the point that this is not an accident or an "oops" on God's part and there is nothing wrong with it.

> I am not focusing on what I don't have and what my marital status is not and being frustrated and wrestling with God. I'm open, clearly if I meet someone that is amazing, but I am not going to wait for my life to start. My life has started, and I am halfway through it. That is what I mean by perspective, I am choosing to and being aware of the opportunities and starting to look for them. I don't want to get to the end of my life and say, I wished my life away.

> In 20s to 25s I missed out a lot of being present because I was so desiring to be married and I missed out being fully immersed in that season of life. You don't know the outcome and if or when you will get married. Be fully present where you are don't waste time on when or who you will marry.

Singles long to be fully present and immersed in their season of singleness. Though for many there is a longing for something else and even at times a bit of disappointment, there is also a great desire to make the most of the life God has given them. Embracing the opportunities that come with singleness is one way that singles find great joy.

SERVE HOWEVER I WANT, WHENEVER I WANT, WHEREVER I WANT

Opportunities certainly abound for those who are single. There is much agreement that one of the major opportunities of being single in ministry is being able to serve however you want, whenever you want, and wherever you want. The freedom to pick up and move to another part of the country or world, to pursue opportunities for ministry both inside and outside the church, to be spontaneous and available to others, and to develop deeper connections with others were among several things mentioned by interviewees.

The idea of being responsible for only yourself and not having to consider someone else affords single staff members a great degree of mobility. There is greater freedom to pick up and go somewhere else with little thought or consideration. Singles aren't held back by the typical things that often anchor married people, like their children's schools or spouse's employment. In addition, there isn't the emotional concern regarding the potential impact a relocation might have on their family. Several singles spoke about the ability to quickly and easily relocate when God presents an opportunity on the other side of the country or the other side of the world.

> I am able to go through open doors that God gives without having to consider other people's schedules. In fact, my current job in Orange County I didn't have to think about relocating my whole family I just had to move myself.

> I have the ability to move quickly because it is just me. I can say "Lord I will go where you want me to go"—I don't have to consider someone else [husband, kids] or how it is going to impact others.

In addition to being able to relocate comes the ability to travel and participate in global ministry endeavors. Many interviewees spoke about foreign travel and missions trips. Whether participating in exploratory trips or leading short- and long-term group trips, the idea of being able to quickly say "yes" to travel, to do so over extended weeks at a time, and even participate in multiple global trips, camps or retreats over a longer period of time was mentioned by many.

> I have been able to go on mission trips to Ghana and didn't have to consider a husband or kids schedule before I decided to go. So being able to serve on global missions whenever I want to is freedom.

> At the last minute I was asked to participate in exploratory trips to Cambodia and India. Because I was single it was easy to say "yes."

> This past summer I was gone about seven weeks out of the summer and I felt the freedom to lead two international trips and be on a houseboat trip with the college students. Being able to do what you want when you want without having to check in with a spouse before saying yes.

Several mentioned the freedom they feel to do ministry even in places that might present more risk. Singles feel less concern for their personal safety since they don't have to worry about something happening to them that would have an impact on their family. There is a willingness to travel to places that pose a greater threat such as third world countries or to do ministry in urban areas such as the inner city among the homeless and addicted populations.

While single staff members still have responsibilities at home, they often find it easier to be flexible with their time and more available to others at a moment's notice. Time is your own when you are single and you get to choose what you spend it on. Singles experience a lot of joy in being able to freely give their time to others. Since many ministry opportunities present themselves at odd hours of the day, night, or weekend, singles find it easier to step up and step in. In addition, being able to be involved in a wide array of ministry opportunities early on allows for increased ministry experience.

> There is one student that lost her mom unexpectedly a year ago and the way I have been able to integrate my life with hers and spend countless hours with her and her family would not have been possible if I had my own family.

> Students can call me, text me, or be around my house all the time. This is unique and doesn't happen a lot. The type of access the high school girls in my life group have is very rare and the capacity to have them around wouldn't be possible if I wasn't single.

> When a student wants to talk at 8:00 pm at night, it is easy for me to talk because I don't have a spouse or kids to worry about.

> My calendar is wide open to meet with people. I can meet with college students and young adults for dinner; I don't have a family schedule to consider. I also think there is a misconception that single people have more time, I have a lot of

responsibilities, but my time is freed up. I am not as bound to a schedule when I am meeting with someone. That is a huge liberty and great opportunity.

Space for extra ministry opportunities like leading worship at an event, don't have to check with someone. This allowed me to get a lot of experience in various ministries early on.

Though singles aren't sure how ministry will change for them if they choose to one day marry, they do sense that it will be different. Some have seen the tension that their married counterparts experience in making both ministry and their families a priority. In fact, to some degree, singles experience this same tension when they are dating someone. In addition, many singles express a willingness and a desire to bless others with their availability of time. They do this by showing up early or staying late at events as a way of helping those who are married and have families.

My availability for students to be a part of their lives, I don't know what that would look like in the future. In my head I think that isn't going to change much, there will still be students at my house all the time, I am still going to be at the things they care about. I don't really have to think let me check my schedule to see what we're doing and if that fits into all these other things students are asking me to do.

I have seen a lot of times with married people that have kids—I notice if they are asked to hang out it is more of a task to work it out with the family schedules. For me I don't have to coordinate anything I just ask do I want to do it. That is a huge blessing I can drop things and move things around at a moment's notice.

I have a lot of friends who are married, with kids, some are in ministry, and I see this "tug" between serving in different ways and the priority of family. In my season of life, I can hang out in a coffee shop and talk with people. I'm not pressed to have to get home. I can also make last minute decisions, not have to check with others—I'm a spontaneous person, could decide to go play basketball, hang out with friends, let's go and do a missions trip.

I have watched youth pastors' spouses struggle with their spouse being in ministry. The spouse would want to take a vacation in summer, but that is the busiest time in youth ministry. If you have a spouse that is on board with ministry, it is easier. I don't think this youth pastor was allowed to accept invitations or do as much outside ministry.

I can show up early and stay late. We have events at all hours and I'm free to come to all of them. When I was dating someone, it was a little harder, [I] had to worry about her as well. I see it as an opportunity to be flexible and do a little extra to help those who are married and have families they are juggling.

Despite the freedom and opportunities for unlimited ministry, singles point out that boundaries are essential. Many described the greater temptation to say "yes" to everything and anyone when you don't have the pressure of a family at home. Though singles enjoy giving of their time, they also recognize that they can be taken advantage of by those who are married.

> Have boundaries. Just because you have time doesn't mean you have to say yes. Know when you have something to give and be aware of what you should give. If you are on a team and everyone should rotate, it shouldn't always be the single person staying the longest. Don't feel guilty for leaving. Boundaries are a lifelong thing for ministry to prevent burnout. Practice it now.

FAMILIES INCLUDE AND CARE FOR YOU

A single person's experience varies depending on how close in proximity they are to their immediate family or whether or not they themselves have children of their own. For many singles, the church becomes their second family and provides a great support for them.

I recall when I (Jane) was single, there were many Sundays after church that I was invited to lunch by families in my church. After a busy morning filled with ministry activity, it was nice to have someone to go to lunch with and talk about the service. On other occasions, I recall being invited into families' homes for dinner. It was a much needed respite from going out to eat or being home alone. This also gave me an opportunity to observe a Christian couple and more fully experience life with kids. In many ways, this helped me to realize how much work it was to be married and more deeply appreciate the joys of my singleness. When I began my graduate program at seminary, a family in the church provided an unsolicited scholarship to me so that I could complete my doctoral work. I definitely felt a greater sense of care and protection by the families in my church because I was single. When I began dating my husband (Gary), one of the elders of the church asked if he could meet with Gary to make sure he was a solid guy. I remember really appreciating that, as my immediate family was out of the area.

Several singles in our research recalled similar experiences of families in their churches looking out for them, inviting them over for meals, including them in their family holidays, providing financial assistance, or simply inviting them to sit with them during church services.

> I used to think people pitied me, but I will take free food. On Mondays, I go to a coworker's house who has a student and we watch "The Bachelor."

> There are some people who are afraid to have me over. I wonder if I was married would I get more invitations for dinner? There are so many that will have me over just as me and I love it they are embracing me as family. I have a friend and we often get invited together, we are both single and even if she can't come, they will still have me over. It has been a joy being in people's homes.

BEING FULLY PRESENT, SINGULARLY FOCUSED

Another joy of being single in ministry is the ability to be fully present and singularly focused. When it comes to being at church events, camps, or retreats, there is a noticeable difference between those who are single and those who are married. Several reflected on the tension that married people appear to experience as they balance family and ministry. The expression "carefree ministry" was used by one of our interviewees as she reflected on the ability to be fully present with no other demands on her attention.

> Events like retreats, I wasn't having to always check in on a spouse while at the retreat. That added a level of being present in the event, I could be 100 percent present. I could give all my attention to the students I didn't feel torn or guilty for not being home.

> I have watched married people at retreats and if their family isn't with them they are on the phone at night checking in with them, if their family is there then they have to spend some time with their spouse and kids and can't be fully present with the students and volunteers.

> It is easier for me to focus as a single person, I don't feel my heart is as pulled worrying about kids or wishing I was at home with my kids. I am able to be fully present and available and give my whole heart to the ministry because it has my undivided attention.

> I think it is a singularity of focus and a singularity of purpose, responsibility. I can work when I want, overwork or underwork. I don't have to add on kids, and other things. I can go and do my job and come home and do what I want. If I want to come home and work I can, there isn't that thing in the back of my mind that says I am responsible to these people and these other things. I don't have those things weighing on my mind. It is very limited, working with people who are married they are not singularly focused, they have way more things going on in their life. They will dump work fast, work is not their priority.

Several singles reflected on the ability to be in the office longer or linger after church events. The gift of presence and not having to rush home to someone or something. A few people reflected on differences they have noticed between marrieds and singles in relation to time, focus, and presence. They find great joy in the singularity of focus they experience as they do ministry.

> I don't have to hurry from work to do something else. The ability to linger creates many opportunities in ministry. You don't have to be anywhere, which allows you to be better at where you are. Such a blessing to be fully where you are and not worried about where you are not.

> When I was single I had more of a one-track mind. Being a husband or wife is a high calling, something I'm always thinking about. When I was single—"whatever someone needed, I would be there." My emotional and full mental focus was devoted to one thing.
>
> The amount of love that I can have for the ministry, for the church as a whole, I don't have to share that with a spouse [God + spouse/kids + ministry vs God + ministry].

Beyond being fully present is the emotional freedom that comes from having a singularity of focus. Singles observe marrieds as often having a sense of urgency to get home to their spouse and kids as they balance ministry and marriage. Marrieds are more likely to feel guilty that they have let someone down or not done enough for their family or for the church. Singles see this tension in those they work with, as related here.

> We have a lot of part-time people and they have commitments to pick up their kids so we have to work our schedules around that and being single I have freedom. I don't have to figure that out. In meetings one of my staff members will look at his phone because of an emergency with his family, I don't have that so I am more present and available.
>
> There isn't the same urgency to get home. This allows for emotional freedom. They think about things like, if I am at an event until 10 pm on a Wednesday night, I won't be home to put my kids to bed. I feel freedom and I don't have the burden of missing out on something or letting my family down.
>
> Logistics of things even like meetings. Even at three o'clock, you see the moms say, "Oh my gosh, I have to go I have carpool." The meeting ends quickly, and we say okay we will talk tomorrow. I don't have to do that.
>
> Since ministry encompasses evenings and weekends, you don't feel guilt for giving up your Saturday. I think married people are often concerned and guilt ridden on weekends.

DEVELOPING DEEPER RELATIONSHIPS WITH GOD AND OTHERS

Another joy and opportunity expressed by many was the ability to develop a deeper relationship with God and others. Singleness allows for the space and margin in life to make these deeper connections. While we all recognize that our most important relationship in life is with God, often the demands of ministry and family responsibilities distract us. Singles appreciate the fact that they can use their time away from ministry to be with God. Instead of juggling children or other family concerns, singles are able to take advantage of the hours before or after work to connect with God. Some churches offer monthly solitude days for staff members and several singles describe these days as more easily embraced by those who are single.

> Number one is being solid in my relationship with God, I don't have anyone else to commune with so by default God is my biggest relationship. It sounds weird, that should be your biggest relationship. I feel so connected to God. I don't have it all figured out. I feel very appreciative of doing life with God and I don't take that for granted. It is one of my greatest joys. We get a solitude day once a month, those days are easy for me to block out, I don't have to check with anyone else's schedule. I will do things like drive up to the mountains and go skiing for the day. I will be on the slopes with piped in worship music talking with God and doing life with Him. I am also leery of possibly I don't want anyone to ever take God's place. I make conscious decisions that God stays in His proper place even if I were to date or get married.

> I can wake up at 5:00 am and spend that time with the Lord and spend three hours getting ready without having to get kids ready or cook for husband.

> One of my joys is having the opportunity on a regular basis to grow deeper in my relationship with God and see how that overflows in my everyday encounters. I can foster an environment to awaken affections for God in leaders and students.

> I can spend more time with God. I have spent weekends and I have struggled with something and I can do the whole weekend of journaling and time with God. I couldn't do that if I had kids. Love to use this time in my life to grow more as a person and especially in my relationship with the Lord.

In addition, ministry is people, and deepening our connections with people takes time. I (Jane) recall fondly leaving the office after a full day of work, picking up KFC, and then heading over to our little league baseball fields, where I would stay all night going from game to game watching the kids in my ministry play baseball. It deepened not only my connection to the kids in my ministry, but also the time in the stands with their parents strengthened my partnership with them.

Similarly, many singles spoke of the opportunity to attend a child's performance, hang out at a student's football game, or sit with an adult at a coffee shop for hours. In addition, many of those interviewed spoke of the opportunity to have students or volunteers in their home or be in the homes of their students and volunteers. Sometimes this includes standing in the gap for a missing parent due to death or divorce. One person in particular spoke about being able to connect with a recent widow. Not only were they able to empathize with the widow's singleness, but they also had the space in their life to make a deeper connection through their interactions with them.

> I get to immerse myself in ministry and spend time with people. I am able to participate in student's lives at a deeper level. I am able to hang out with them and have them at my house.
>
> I know of a few people that have experienced the death of their spouse in the last year or two and watching them adjust to that and we have an interesting connection because we are both single. I get to love on them.
>
> Pouring into students, I've been able to create space and time in my schedule to spend time with students—only because I'm single. One student lost her mom a year ago, I've been able to integrate her life with mine, would not have been possible if I had my own family. Most of my time is spent at work, with friends, and with students. Most of my weekends are spent with students—call me, text me, be around me at my house. The amount of access my high school life group girls have—rare.

Singles also talk about the ability to connect more deeply with friends and coworkers after work. As one person described, "It is easy to connect with single friends and coworkers after work, but those who are married have to go pick up the kids from day care, can't because their spouse is out of town, or have to check with their spouse first." Singles have the freedom to be more socially connected with others. It isn't that married people aren't social, but it takes more intentional planning and there are a lot of competing priorities.

BEING ABLE TO BE GENEROUS

Though singles admit that this is a season in their life when they can be more inward focused, they also recognize that it is a time in which they can choose to be more generous. One of the opportunities of only having yourself to care for is the ability to give more to others. Several shared that they find joy in deciding where to give, when to give, and who to give support to without having to consult with a spouse. Though many singles echoed that being single often means you aren't paid as much and have limited financial resources, it also means that you have fewer financial responsibilities both now and in the future.

> I can give of my finances to whatever I want without thinking, "Oh I can't do that, I have to save for my kid's college tuition."
>
> I am able to use my money in the way I feel God would have me use it. I have the freedom to save, to spend, to invest, and to give. I determine where and when I want to give of my finances.

In addition to financial generosity, singles find joy in being generous with their time. This is especially seen in their attitude toward serving and supporting those who are married in ministry. It is also seen in volunteering their time outside their own ministry responsibilities and being more involved in the life of the church.

> Every Christmas Eve I love to release my team. Yes, I have Christmas Eve plans and I have extended family that I go and spend time with. I don't have littles at home and my team members that do have kids, I love to let them go and be with their family. People work so hard and that is something where on a team your leader is saying, "I want to do this for you," and I get to serve other people through that. I enjoy that and it is fun. We make a lot of hard asks and this allows me to bless them.
>
> One of my staff members has two kids so they get sick and there are challenges that she has, she has even called me to watch her kids so she can get to a staff meeting. So, childcare is an issue at times. Being able to house sit or kid sit for families is such an opportunity to serve them.
>
> I have more energy and I'm not being tied down to someone else's schedule. I don't have to think about anyone else's needs or feelings, so I do more. If the church doors are open, I am there. I attend every event at the church and all the services. I volunteer outside my ministry responsibilities. More of the older married folks are selective in what they volunteer for.

BEING ABLE TO REST AND RENEW

There is much agreement that being at home represents different things to singles and marrieds. For the most part, while singles still have responsibilities at home, they describe home as a haven, a place of retreat and rest. In contrast, they recognize that a married person leaves work only to return home to what might be an even bigger and more demanding job. Days off also look different for a single person. Singles often describe their days off as time to do whatever they want, an opportunity to rejuvenate and recharge. Many describe this ability to rest as a benefit to their physical endurance, mental stamina, and spiritual life.

> There are times when I go home alone, and I know I can truly rest, but others have to go home and take care of kids and family. I have freedom to go home and do what I want to do. I can unwind and rest. I have married people tell me how lucky I am to be able to do this.
>
> I can be home and sit and read my book and drink my coffee and not be bothered. I can take time to rest and do whatever I need for my soul to be well. I'm an introvert I need to be by myself to reenergize, I love the beach. I love to read and stay home and just be in the quiet with the Lord.

> I have been able to do and see things that I wouldn't have done if I was married it has been a blessing. I have traveled the world and gone to parts of the world that most people don't have the time and money to see. I can be sporadic and go on hikes after work. I am an adventurous person and that speaks loudly to me I have just packed up and gone places when I wanted.
>
> I know when I walk in through the door of my house it is just me and I can unplug and just rest. If I want to cook or eat fast food or make a seven course meal my evenings are my own. My day off I am in my pajamas most of the day, the rest and recharging is complete rest if I want it to be. Hanging out with friends, having people over. I love that when I am done I am done and I am not going from one job to the other.

In addition to rest, several singles pointed out the opportunity to grow and develop new skills. Whether pursuing new hobbies, spending personal time studying, or pursuing a graduate degree program, singleness affords greater opportunity for personal growth.

> I have the ability to pursue my own interests like learning to play the piano. I am able to practice late at night. I can try new hobbies and learn new skills because I have the time and space to do it.
>
> Ability to learn at a rapid pace. Some evenings I go home and pour into a book, study for four to five hours, without it getting in the way of other work during the day or my relationships at home.
>
> I am in seminary and because I am single I have the freedom to work full time and go to school part time. I think if I got married my life would look different—I would have to spend time on the relationship. If you want to do graduate school and you are single then do it. You can have your Master's degree and not have to balance work, school and marriage.

BEING SINGLE AS A PLATFORM FOR MINISTRY

Many singles reflected on how their own singleness becomes part of their ministry. Since our congregations are made up of both marrieds and singles, being single on staff is an opportunity to be a voice for other singles in the church and broader community. It is also an opportunity for others to see the restorative process of God's grace at work through situations like divorce. One interviewee reflected on her own journey of becoming divorced while in ministry.

> A memory came back, when I returned to my home church in 2000 as a single mom, I had two kids in second grade. I thought, "There is no church going to hire me back. I am cursed." And the fact that they would hire me—I thought,

> "God, you're not done with me I am not on the shelf." It was so affirming I didn't know that would become my platform or message. I had been gone for twelve years from that church, single moms are everywhere at the church and I come in as the Children's Pastor as a single mom. One day this mom comes in with three little boys, and she starts weeping and she said, "The fact that you are here as a staff person lets me know it's okay to be here at church." Since that day, I have met many single moms. It is like if you have a special needs child then you have that ministry. You didn't ask for that ministry, but God uses it. So, I started a single mom's small group and it blossomed into a ministry.

Others shared about the opportunities they have had as a single staff person to teach or preach in large group settings, whether at a women's ministry event or from the pulpit. The voice of a single person isn't always heard in these forums. Singles provide a different perspective on life and also serve as a role model for others in the church. Since most pastors are married, having a single person on staff allows the congregation to see what it is like to be a Christ follower who is single. Those who are single are relatable to a large demographic in our church that is often under represented.

> For me, it has been pouring into young adults and college students and speaking at events. I spoke at a women's event, speaking about being single. There are so many people out there who are single, 50 percent of the community are single, not necessarily the church but in our culture. It has given me a platform. At my church, I get to preach and my first sermon I talked about the waiting game and how I am waiting for that in my singleness. Two years later people still come up to me and remember that. I have spoken in our high school group about it, and other opportunities to identify with people in that same venue. Whether they are never married or single again. I always thought I would be married in my late twenties and starting a family, but that wasn't what God had for me, so to speak out of a heart of contentment and peace has been impactful since I am on staff at the church and this is my journey.

> Being able to represent the single voice in the community. So many of the top leaders are married and have lost the perspective of someone single. Whether it is in sermon preparation or an event being hosted by the church, I am able to provide a different perspective on how that might impact someone who is single.

> It was more real to talk about dating and sex issues because that is where I was as well. I was in the same boat as them for so long. They got to see a single youth pastor with a desire to be married who was able to live my own advice—biblical advice.

Singles enjoy the freedom they have to serve however, whenever, and wherever they want. They speak of being unencumbered, single-focused, and fully available to invest deeply in their relationship with God and others.

They sense a greater capacity to be more generous with their time and their finances. They find great joy in being able to have space for rest and renewal. Many see their singleness as a platform to minister to other singles in the church and recognize that they serve as a role model of what it means to follow Jesus as a single person. Singles that embrace the opportunities of this season experience great joy in the journey.

QUESTIONS FOR REFLECTION AND DISCUSSION

There are many joys and opportunities that come with serving on a church staff as a single person. For some it is easier to see the challenges than the opportunities. The questions that follow are designed to help you think through your own experiences and surface ideas that might help you savor the joys of this season of your life and ministry. We would encourage you to find a close friend or colleague with whom you feel comfortable sharing, as these may be good questions to discuss together.

1. Take some time to think about the joys and opportunities you have experienced as a single staff member. Make a list of things you are grateful for in this season of life. How might you keep this in a prominent place as a reminder and source of encouragement?
2. Knowing that singles have greater mobility and freedom to travel, are there places that you would like to go, mission trips you would like to be a part of, or ministry opportunities you would like to pursue? What draws you to these places? What holds you back from pursuing these things? Who can you share these dreams with?
3. Have you considered what you will give up if you choose to get married? What are some of the things that would change for you? What are you able to do now that those who are married in ministry find more challenging to do? In what ways might you take full advantage of this season of life?
4. How is your relationship with God? How do you connect best with God? What other relationships in your life need to be deepened? What patterns in your life need to change in order for you to prioritize these relationships and ensure they are not crowded out by a busy schedule?
5. In what ways might you be generous with your time by volunteering in ministries inside or outside your church? In what ways might you be able to bless and encourage a colleague in ministry by being generous with your time?
6. What type of things brings you rest and renewal? How are you spending your time off? What is something you would like to pursue or accomplish in the area of personal development?

7. How might you be a voice in your church for those who are single? How might you use your singleness as a platform for ministry to others?

Ideas for Discussion with Your Ministry Supervisor

1. In what ways might our church utilize singles in more prominent volunteer and leadership roles, especially roles that require flexibility in time commitment or travel?
   Are there ministry opportunities inside or outside the church that you would like to pursue?
2. How are we doing as a church caring for and including you in our families? How could some of our families better support and encourage you?
3. What can supervisors do to help singles establish better ministry boundaries and create margin for rest and renewal?
4. In what ways might our church unintentionally place higher expectations on those who are single in ministry? What patterns need to change?
5. How might our church encourage and support your personal growth and development?
6. Are we creating opportunities for the single voice to be heard in our congregation? How might we better utilize your voice for those who are single in our church and community? What would be the value of doing that more?

Chapter 2

The Challenges of Being a Single Ministry Staff Member in a "Family Church"

"When are you going to get married?" People ask those questions, and I don't think their intentions are bad, but it makes it seem like it's an expectation or an aspect of life that I have to pursue, and being single is not an okay option. . . . Is it okay to be single, and for that to be respected?

THE NORMALIZATION OF MARRIAGE IN THE CHURCH

So far, we've looked at the opportunities and joys of ministry while single. These are things to give thanks for and to savor. However, one of the clearest, strongest themes that we heard from the men and women that we interviewed was that it can also be very challenging being a staff member in the church when you are single. One of the primary reasons for these challenges seems to be that our churches, much like the cultures that surround them, have certain social expectations of adults, and one of the stronger ones that shapes how we think about our lives is a belief that most people ought to be, and ought to want to be, married. To not be married, or to not be actively seeking a marriage partner, is seen as abnormal, a sign that something is wrong. Over and over again, both men and women shared how their being single causes others to question their value, wholeness, trustworthiness, and maturity. This is true in general for North American church settings and can be even more keenly felt in some immigrant church settings. Here are several examples of the comments we heard from their experience:

> My first day here was on a Sunday and our Spanish-speaking service straight up asked me if I was married, and I said "No, I'm single." This was in front of their church—so they prayed for my spouse right there. . . .

> When I did get married, people said "Finally!" "What do you mean 'Finally'?" "Finally" is kind of offensive, because it was like I had finally arrived to this stage in life where I can talk this talk with everybody else.
>
> Staff members and congregants, they view you as incomplete until you have a spouse. They view you as, "Oh, you're a work in progress," until you get a significant other, and then, once you are there, it is like you have reached some kind of mountaintop deal, which is ridiculous in and of itself.
>
> A lot of people believe you are not complete without a spouse, or are with someone, and whether they will say that explicitly or not is irrelevant, but that's what they are communicating to you.
>
> If you are a healthy Christian, you should get married. The end. If not, then something is wrong with you. What normal man would not want to get married?

This elevation of the status of marriage can come close to a kind of idolatry, assuming that marriage is the greater good for everyone's lives, a sign of God's blessing and reward, and a reassurance of a person's "normality." After all, what normal man (or woman) doesn't want to be married? If they do want this, then it seems to be a mark of failure if time goes by and it is not happening, that something is wrong with the person. Many single women and men shared how they felt judged for being single, particularly as they got older, and feeling somehow "behind" developmentally if they weren't married by a certain age. Some have even had their sexual orientation questioned. Here is some of what we heard from those we interviewed.

> There's a prevalence of the perceptions that as a single person you are more prone to sexual sin. You're more available, more free, less mature, those kinds of conceptions have swirled around. . . .
>
> At some point, they ask "Why are you still single?" Is there something wrong? I think there's that negative connotation of if you are single for so long, why are you single? "Are you gay, and you don't admit it? Is that why?"
>
> I think that single women, particularly if they are single and younger, they are treated more cautiously, more protectively, and sometimes like they are more dangerous. . . . So, couples who are willing to invite a single over—typically it is easier to invite a man than a female, . . . There still lives that sense of fear of Tertullian, and that we're all seductresses.
>
> I think the biggest thing is people constantly reminding me that I'm single. "Oh, when are you going to get married?" I don't have that timeline in my head. I did have a timeline in my head and in *my* timeline, I was married ten years ago, and obviously that didn't pan out.

THE PERCEIVED IMMATURITY AND INCOMPLETENESS OF SINGLE ADULTS IN MINISTRY

One of the ways that the prevalent cultural expectation of marriage is expressed is in how some parents of children participating in the church's children and youth ministries treat and interact with ministry staff members who are single. Parents can have a harder time entrusting their children to the care of single men and women staff members rather than married ones, concerned that the staff member may not be mature enough to handle the ministry responsibility with their child. Two excerpts from the interviews capture this well.

> I work with a very young generation, and like I said, not a lot of guys do that. And so, when the parents come and they drop off their kid and they see a single, college aged guy, there's not a lot of good ideas of what single guys of my age do, there's a lot of concerns. I feel like people don't trust men, and don't trust single men to be with kids. . . . I get looks.

> There's an underlying pressure. If you're not married, honestly, you're not considered an adult. . . . If you're not married, it equals being less mature. . . . I feel it more, I would say, with parents of students, actually. I think any time you have younger staff members who are in their twenties, . . . parents of students feel like you are too young to be caring for my student, when they initially meet you. I think there is something about if you are wearing a wedding ring that instantly makes them think, "Well, they're old enough to be married, so they're old enough to care for my child."

Somehow, the younger single adult may not be viewed as "fully adult" yet, needing to prove his or her responsibility and maturity. This attitude may take some time to overcome as the single staff member serves in leadership roles, with parents watching and looking for signs of responsibility or irresponsibility. Interestingly enough, this attitude can quickly change if the staff member begins to date someone steadily, or gets engaged, and it definitely changes if they get married. Now they have "arrived," showing responsibility and maturity by leaving their single life behind for a marriage relationship. Several of the staff members who dated steadily or got married while in ministry reported how people's attitudes toward them changed almost overnight. Here is what some of them said about their experience:

> Everyone loves a wedding! It was like overnight, people saw me as a different person. I very clearly remember all of a sudden people looked at me as more responsible, they looked at me as having things more figured out, and I'm like, "Two days ago I had nothing figured out to you, and now a week later I have it figured out?"

> It's like, when you get married, you age five years overnight to people, you know. So immediately it was, I experienced people seeing me as more mature, as more competent. . . . My competency didn't change, but the trust level of my competence did, which was strange.

> I feel like there is a big gap between married people . . . because you are perceived as more mature, you are perceived as having your life together. [For singles] that does not go away unless you try and do your best to sway them, to show them that you are responsible, show you are mature, show what you've got.

> I had a friend who came on staff who was in a very serious relationship, and they were like, "Oh, they're about to get engaged, about to get married." I think the perception of him was really different than the perception of me . . . and the treatment and respect that he got from others and staff members was different from the way I got it.

One other way that parents communicate this perception of immaturity is when interacting with single staff members about the needs of their children. Too often, the parent dismisses the concerns, views, and ideas of the single staff member, or the parent doesn't view the staff member as having anything valuable to share because of their lack of experience as parents. It can take significant time to overcome this hurdle, but many single staff members have done it, and their perspectives on ministry with children and youth are respected and highly valued. But this can be a real struggle. As one female staff member shared:

> I've had parents ask me, "Do you have kids?" [because we're in the midst of discussing a discipline issue]. "Well, do you have kids?" I feel like it's an instant shutdown on any credibility I might have, and any possible conversation, so it's just like, "And, we're done."

This experience can be a bit different for single women and men staff members. Single women report that because they have not yet had children themselves, some mothers may question their ability to care for children in the church, but if they serve in youth ministry they are more often seen as potential mentors, big sister figures for the female youth, and that is valued and appreciated. For single men on staff, this can be more challenging. They are often not viewed as good candidates for children's ministry, sometimes actually viewed as potential risks for youth ministry, particularly if they are young. Are they really mature enough to care for someone else's children? Some parents are also concerned about possible sexual abuse or inappropriate relationships developing between their daughters and the single male staff member. This kind of fear can make it harder for a single male staff member to gain parental trust. In some cases, it may never really go away until he marries.

SINGLENESS SEEN AS A PROBLEM TO FIX

In many of the interviews with single church staff members, we heard descriptions of their interaction with congregation members, showing that many people had a genuine and deep appreciation, love, and care for the single staff member. These church members thought highly of them and saw them as gifted and caring people they enjoyed being around. They felt close to them and wanted what would be best for them, which too often translated into a desire to see them get married. Here are some reflections from a few of those we interviewed about this issue.

> Sometimes people don't know what to do with someone who is single. I get people coming into my office who say, "I don't get it, you're so nice, and you're so caring, like, why are you single?" And I'm like, "What?" Some of them will say, "You are really pretty, why are you single?" . . . Sometimes that's a challenge where you feel like this alien life form that people don't understand, especially if you are very focused and know that God has not called you to that.

> I think they can sympathize with, "Oh, I'm just still waiting," or "I haven't found someone," and they feel like, "Oh, I can help find someone," but it's even weirder I think for others when they're like, "Oh, you're not called [to be married]? That's weird, who would not be called to be married?"

> "We've got to set you up with somebody," as if there was a problem to be fixed. I would watch, especially some of the guys who were single; they would feel like something was wrong with them, because "I haven't figured it out." Then to hear the narrative of someone who's married, "You are so great, why aren't you married? Why is this not happening? We love that you are here. Why aren't you married?" Isn't it enough that we are here and we have the ability to do what we can do because we are created in this way?

> "Oh, I know this great guy you should date, or "I wish I knew someone that you could date." It comes from this sweet part of their heart. It's like, they look at you, they talk with you, and they're like, "You're so great, like you should be with someone." I don't know what that way of thinking is, but, Jesus was so great, why wasn't He with anyone? Just because you're a great person and you have a lot to offer doesn't mean that you have to offer it in a relationship that is a romantic one.

One of the relational dynamics that can develop in church ministry settings is a natural expression of the unity and family-like relationship we have as the Body of Christ or the family of God. As our relationships grow closer, we feel freer to talk about more personal things and sometimes to offer advice, whether asked for or not. For the church staff member, it can be quite natural for many people to feel close enough to them to ask about and comment on their personal lives. It can be a healthy sign of good relationships, but it can also be challenging if some begin taking on a fatherly or motherly role, offering advice when it has not been asked for. (As a father of adult children, I'm sometimes reminded that unsolicited advice is frequently received as criticism.) In family settings, it is quite natural for family members to ask each other personal questions, to "get in each other's business." Single church staff members who have been successful in developing relationships with others in the church may find their personal lives receiving a lot of attention—the proverbial "goldfish bowl" experience, where everyone seems aware of what is going on, and some may feel free to offer advice. Unfortunately, one of the issues that can receive a lot of attention is the perceived "problem" of the staff member's singleness that needs to be "fixed." Many of those we interviewed recognized that this kind of concern came from a genuine desire to see them happy, but it was still challenging to receive. Here are a few reflections that illustrate this well.

> You almost become a project of all of the other married people. Who can I set this guy up with? My first two weeks on the job, my boss at the time asked, "So, who are you dating? Who are you interested in?" I just got here!

> It's very interesting, people are always trying to marry you off. Everyone knows someone that I should date. . . . You can be totally secure in your singleness, but somehow all the people around you are not secure in your singleness. It's a lot of conversations to assure them that you are okay. But it is frustrating constantly going back and forth of "I'm not a project."

> It's the bigger, "This is a problem to be fixed" situation. "We're going to try and figure out why it is that you're not married and how, is it something you're doing, is it the way you're dressing, the way you're talking? Maybe you're too intimidating, maybe you need to make more time for this, like you need to give more attention to this. Do online dating." It's like everyone has a solution for everything.

> Within the span of one week, I was asked if I was dating three times, and when I said "No," it was like a disappointment, and then one of them actually lectured me on it, and I was like, "Excuse you?" . . . I don't feel like I have to defend why I'm single. We need to make singleness acceptable and okay.

This kind of concern often leads to congregation members playing matchmaker, trying to set the staff member up with someone else they know in hopes that both will enjoy the relationship. Unfortunately, it can create awkward situations if the staff member declines to follow up on the recommendation or if they do go out with the person but decide it was not a relationship they want to pursue further. It can be hard to explain why it did not work out to the one who set them up. Some examples of this challenge were shared with us.

> There are a lot of matchmakers in the church, and that's probably true outside the church too. . . . There's a lot of that, and feelings of discomfort when you tell someone, "I'm not interested in meeting your friend. I'm sure she's great, but that's not where I am right now."

> At least two women at church have said, "How come you are not married? Can I introduce you to a friend of mine?" So, there's always that perception that it would be better if you were married. I'm sure they have good intentions. It's always, "You're a good guy, let me introduce you to a good friend of mine."

> I do get that pressure a lot at church. It is what it is, people do mean well, both for you and for their other friend that they're trying to get set up with someone, so to some degree I appreciate it. I think the few times where it's gotten not good is when people consistently pester me about it. And it can get awkward too when someone presents someone to you that you're just not interested in at all.

As a few of our interviewees commented, you can feel very secure in your singleness, that it is what God has for you, at least at this time of your life, but it may be hard for others around you to have that same sense of security.

THE MARKETING AND MINISTRY OF THE "FAMILY CHURCH"

Many churches work hard to promote their ministries to families, emphasizing their children and youth ministries, having classes, retreats, and sermon series on marriage and parenting relationships, and organizing small groups for couples. Websites often show smiling families, communicating that this is a place where families are welcome, and ministries are organized for those who are married, but what about for those who are single?

In many churches, single adults feel overlooked, including those who serve on staff. There may be a college or "young adult" ministry, but for those who get a little older and remain single, most churches do not seem to know what to do with them. As an adult Bible study leader, I was once approached by a church staff member, who urged me to have our group do a marriage-enrichment study, and I had to remind him that we had several singles in our group who would not find that helpful. Somehow, this had not occurred to him. It was as if the singles were invisible.

Some churches offer singles' ministries, but most of the single church staff members who spoke of these ministries at their churches said they felt like "meat markets," where singles went until they found someone to date and then no longer attended, or that they attracted too many singles with social challenges, making the groups dysfunctional and unattractive to other singles. Several shared that their churches, which had large singles' ministries in the past, were no longer offering singles' ministries, and that this was true of other churches in their area as well.

> Single ministries in every church that I've been a part of suck! Like, they're not even okay, they suck. They're either nonexistent, or at best they'll have a college ministry or a college and just out of college ministry and they'll call that their singles' ministry. And if they have anything [else], it will be for people in their late fifties and sixties who are single . . . and there is nothing for the people in between.

> If there was a place [at my church] that was for single people I would be a little hesitant to go to that because it would feel a little bit like a "meat market" or really isolated as a single person, because I think there is a balance, like if I were to be isolated as a single person, that doesn't feel good, like "Here, put a target on my back or a stamp on my forehead that I'm single. . . .

> Being single in the church is hard because few want to put any resources towards it. And then if you do try to do something it attracts the more outskirts of people because maybe it's gotten such a bad rap. . . . I think it's hard to find healthy post-college years or early twenties, it's tough to find that just in general in churches.

For too many churches, singles, including singles who serve on church staff, are overlooked in ministry design, or the ministries developed are not supporting and affirming them as single disciples of Christ. Instead, cultural expectations expressed by church members regarding the normality of marriage can challenge their sense of completeness in Christ. What many told us was that their churches needed a clearer and stronger theology of singleness, one that recognized one's wholeness in relationship with Christ, ability to mature as they walked with Christ, giftedness for ministry, and valued place in the Body of Christ. Until this is addressed, singles in the church, both congregation members and church staff, will continue to feel like they don't quite fit, that there is something wrong with them, and they are not okay the way they are. In addition, as a couple of our interviewees noted, if our churches are to call our brothers and sisters who experience same-sex attraction to a life of celibacy, we have to create an environment in the church where singles are accepted, valued, and included in the life of the church, that they are not viewed as incomplete in Christ, and that singleness is not seen as a problem to be fixed.

WHAT YOU CAN DO TO IMPROVE YOUR SITUATION

In the chapters that follow, we will be exploring some of the bigger personal challenges that singles in ministry often face and ways of responding that can help you thrive in ministry. This chapter has focused on a foundational issue of how singles are often perceived and responded to in a church culture that focuses heavily on marriage and family ministries. While we may not be able to change the culture our churches are immersed in, we *can* begin to change the culture of our churches to better reflect God's perspectives and values. This is best pursued through a combination of good teaching and the examples of single lives, well lived. Here are seven ideas you might consider to help your church better support their single staff members and other singles in the church as well.

Be Secure in Who and Whose You Are

Because of our cultural valuing of marriage, whether you are open to dating and marriage, or are convinced that God has called you to remain single, at least for now, you run the risk of being misunderstood or judged by members of your congregation. It is important, therefore, that you have a strong sense of security in who God made you to be, and your wholeness in your relationship with God through Christ Jesus. You are loved, accepted, and valued by the God who made and redeemed you, and who called and equipped you to serve His church. You are a significant part of the Body of Christ, gifted and able to be a channel of God's grace to others (1 Peter 4:10), and someone who benefits from the ministry and gifting of others. Whether single or married, this truth does not change. Take time to read and meditate on those portions of Scripture that affirm who you are in Christ, and that He is the one who makes you whole and able to serve.

Affirm the Significance of Singleness in Adult Discipleship

Where you have opportunity, encourage your church to teach about the value and importance of following Christ as a single person. In committee and board meetings, when you see that the concerns seem narrowly focused on couples or families, give gentle reminders of the many in the church who are single who also need support, encouragement, and teaching on how to follow Christ in all of their life. If you notice that sermon illustrations seem to focus mainly on marriage or family contexts, encourage your pastor(s) to think about ways to apply their messages to those who are single, whether young or old, never married, divorced or widowed. Affirm and thank them when they do. If your church sponsors couples' retreats or marriage or parenting seminars, raise the possibility of seminars or retreats for singles in different life situations as well (e.g., men, women, younger, older, widowed, or divorced). Their needs are just as real those of married couples, and these can be good outreach events for your church members to invite friends to participate in as well. We sometimes forget that Jesus was single, the marital status of many of his disciples is not known to us, and that Paul was single. What might others who are single learn from some focused study on their lives and ministry? What might the whole church learn about the significance of the single life from this kind of study?

Affirm Your Church's Ministry with Couples and Families

None of those we interviewed felt a need to reduce their church's emphasis on helping couples have strong marriages or families. The need for these kinds of ministries is clear in our society where marriage relationships are often strained and broken and families struggle with multiple challenges. As a ministry leader in your church, be clear in your support for the full range of ministries going on with couples and families, and do what you can to be of practical help. Your concern for the well-being and support of couples and families in your church sets an example for others and encourages others to think beyond their own needs. Encourage others who are single to join you in volunteering at ministry events to allow couples and parents to participate together. Whether it is in helping with registrations, welcoming, refreshments, childcare, or in other ways, your demonstrated support for couples and families in your church can be a blessing to them, and it is a way of living out the mutual care of the Body of Christ. Demonstrate that your concerns are for the whole Body and not just for those who are single like you.

Promote Mixed Ministry Opportunities

There is a great temptation in church ministry, particularly in larger churches, that when we identify an area of ministry need, we tend to create a group to address it and then assume the needs of these people are now met. Do we have single mothers in our church? If so, let's create a single mothers' group. Do we have a lot of college students? Then, let's create a college group. Do we have people struggling with addictions? Let's have a recovery group. This kind of ministry approach, as well intentioned and helpful as it is, can unintentionally contribute to the fracturing and isolation of the church, creating "ministry silos," hindering the mutual ministry of the Body of Christ as a whole. These kinds of focused ministry efforts must be balanced with a rich interactional congregational life across generations and life situations. As Paul wrote in 1 Corinthians 12, the eyes need the hands, the head needs the feet, and we are to have "the same care for one another" (v. 25). While different groups of people can benefit from some focused ministry attention, the church will experience stronger, long-term health when we also have much of our time together, carrying out mutual care and ministry.

Encourage the development of small groups that include both married and single adults, younger and older, so that they can learn from and encourage one another. Intergenerational groups involving children and youth, as well, can be wonderful opportunities for mutual ministry, whether long term or for certain seasons of the year (e.g., Advent, Lent, Summer). If the church has a young adult group, encourage them to invite a seniors group to join them for an evening of fun, sharing and prayer together. When we do these kinds of things, it helps people to get to know people whose life situations are different from their own, and it grows not only our sense of oneness in the Body of Christ but also our appreciation of and care for one another.

Work at Being Known and Earn Respect over Time

I think we have to face it, given our cultural emphasis on marriage and parenting, singles, especially those who are younger, will not automatically be viewed as mature and responsible, even if they have ministry training and serve on church staffs. Some of those we interviewed reported that they felt respected and that their leadership within their ministry areas was supported and valued. A closer look at these people shows that they have been in their ministry roles for a few years, and some of them grew up in the church and have been known by the members of their congregation for years. It takes time to overcome stereotypes and prejudices—time spent demonstrating maturity, trustworthiness, care for others, and humility.

Two things stand out that are worth investing in over the long haul. First, take the initiative to help others get to know you and see your heart for ministry and your willingness to take on responsibility. For those who work in children or youth ministry, this means taking time to talk with parents, being available to interact with them before and after ministry sessions, inviting parents to meet with the ministry staff to share your passion and vision for ministry, and allowing them to get to know you better. Send out newsletters to share what is going on and your vision for ministry. When you are together, listen well, and show that you understand their concerns and are doing your best to address them. If invited to their homes, go, and let them get to know you outside of the ministry setting. Work at building mutually respectful relationships with them and affirm them whenever you can—parenting is a 24/7 challenge!

Second, don't assume that this kind of appreciation and respect will happen overnight. Earning respect takes time, so view this as a long-term investment through faithfulness in ministry. As time goes by, and parents see your consistent responsibility and care for others and a willingness to listen and learn from others, their views of you will change. The more they get to know you, and the better you demonstrate your responsiveness and trustworthiness, the sooner their concerns will fade and you will become someone they deeply appreciate and want to support.

Be Clear and Gracious When Responding to Would-Be Matchmakers

It may be hard at times, but try to remember that if some church members ask about your dating life, or try to set you up for a date with someone they know, it generally comes out of a heart that desires something good for you and for the person they are trying to interest you in. They may think so highly of you, and wish their friend could know someone like you. It may still be frustrating, but try to recognize the intent as well as you can. That said, it can help if you find a way to clearly let people know whether or not you welcome these kinds of inquiries and recommendations or if you simply are not looking to date at this time. When asked, find a gracious way to let them know if you are open or if you prefer to not pursue this now. Several of the single staff members we talked with, both men and women, said that there were times when they did appreciate this kind of interest in their personal lives and welcomed it from those they knew well and knew were desiring their best. Some of the singles, particularly some who were older, expressed concern that no one asked them about their dating any more, or ever recommended someone to them they might want to get to know. It was as if no one expected them "at their age" to still be interested in dating—but they were! They felt overlooked, as if others had given up on them in this area of their life. Find ways to let others who ask know if you appreciate their recommendations or if your contentment with your singleness is such that you really don't want to explore these kinds of dating opportunities.

Let Your Supervisor or Support Team Know Where You Need Support

We'll be saying more about staff relationships later, but for now let me highlight one important aspect of your working relationship with your supervisor and any support team you may have. Don't expect them to know what frustrations or struggles you are facing or feeling, or the kind of support you would appreciate. They are not mind readers, and many of us communicate such an air of confidence and capability that it can surprise those we work with when we finally share that we are struggling with something. Work on building the kind of relationship with your supervisor and/or your support team where you are able to honestly share if something is troubling you, or if you would appreciate something but it feels hard to ask for. If you are living alone, and you would value an evening spent having dinner and watching a show or movie or playing a game with the family of someone you work with, let them know. If a holiday is coming up and you haven't seen your parents or extended family in some time and would appreciate time off to be able to visit them, ask if your ministry responsibilities can be shifted to give you the freedom to do this. If you are feeling like some in the congregation are questioning your maturity and responsibility, talk over ideas for what might help change these attitudes. Don't feel that you have to solve these things on your own. This is what the mutual ministry of the Body of Christ is for—mutual care for one another.

QUESTIONS FOR REFLECTION AND DISCUSSION

Serving on church staff as a single person brings wonderful blessings and real challenges, but every church situation and everyone's experience is different. The questions that follow are designed to help you think through your own experiences and surface ideas that might serve to improve your situation and how you respond to the challenges you face. If you have friends you feel comfortable sharing closely with, these may be good questions to discuss together.

1. Take some time to think about the range of ministries going on in your church and the ways in which you see how the church welcomes and values single adults, or ways in which you see them overlooked or marginalized. What do you think is worthy of affirmation and celebration? What do you think needs more thoughtful attention? How does this impact you, personally, as you serve in a ministry role?
2. How do you cope or respond if/when expectations of marriage as a goal are emphasized in your congregational setting? How does this impact your feelings about your singleness and your walk with God? What are you doing to remind yourself of your wholeness in Christ and God's love and acceptance?
3. Have you found any ways to help church leaders give better attention to the needs of single adults in your congregation? What might you consider doing to build greater understanding of these needs and a desire to address them?
4. Have you found a "mixed" group of adults to be involved with, or do you prefer gathering with other singles? What are you looking for from the group(s) you are currently participating in? What do you think you need?
5. How are you taking the initiative in helping congregation members, particularly those involved in or impacted by your ministry area, in getting to know you? How are you investing in good communication and consistent actions to build credibility and respect if some have not been quick to give this?
6. What do you say when others ask about your dating or try to set you up on a date? How do you feel about this kind of inquiry into your personal life? If no one is asking you about this, how do you feel about that lack of inquiry?

7. Who are you sharing your concerns and needs with? To what degree do you feel comfortable sharing personal issues with your supervisor? If this does not feel comfortable, who is there on your support team that you can do this with?

Ideas for Discussion with Your Ministry Supervisor

1. What is our church doing to help those who are single connect well within the church and feel included and supported in their life situations?
2. What are we doing that may inadvertently make single adults feel that they are odd for not being married?
3. What are we doing to affirm the significance of singleness for discipleship, to promote wholehearted commitment to follow Christ and to use the opportunities that being single can give for ministry and growth opportunities?
4. How do people tend to respond to single staff members in the church? What could be done to promote an appreciation of their ministry strengths and greater respect for them as gifted ministers?
5. What does the way we market the church and its ministries say about who the church is for? Is our family-friendly message so strong that it is drowning out our broader message of the church being for people of all ages and stages of life?
6. Are we creating ministry silos that keep singles from being more naturally involved in the full range of the church's ministries? How are we connecting them with other adults who are married and in different life situations? What would be the value of doing that more?

Chapter 3

Dating in the Fishbowl

> *Dating is a challenge. People think, "Oh, you're in this world where you're exposed to so many people so of course you're going to find a great guy. You're going to find a great guy so quickly." And I would say that the number one deterrent to a dating scenario is when they ask what you do for a living.*

Not every staff member who is single is looking for a romantic relationship or to find a marriage partner. Many are content being single, at least for now, and feel that life is full and complete without looking for this kind of relationship. But for those who are open to the possibility of dating, or who actively desire it, dating as a church staff member is one of the more challenging experiences they face. The challenges begin with thinking about whom to date and how to meet them, how congregation members respond when the staff member is dating, and many issues related to how to navigate the dating relationship in the midst of ministry demands. Among those we interviewed, both younger and older single ministry staff persons talked about the challenges of dating, but older single ministry staff persons sometimes spoke with a greater sense of concern or frustration. While being a single staff member in a church has its challenges, the pursuit of dating relationships can be even more so.

WHO SHOULD I DATE? HOW CAN I MEET THEM?

Finding someone to date as an adult can be hard enough all on its own, but when you are a church staff member it becomes even more challenging.

On the one hand, some people are attracted to someone they perceive as spiritually mature and caring, a leader of others. There can even be a hint of "celebrity" for those in public ministry, and they may find themselves receiving attention from some eligible singles in the church, or the siblings or parents of eligible singles ("Pastor, I'd like to introduce you to my younger sister . . ."). On the other hand, dating a church staff member may not sound appealing to some people, assuming that the life of a church staff member means they are always on call, or they don't enjoy going to parties, or are not fun to be around. In addition, people with church experience know that most church staff members don't earn much and may not view them as being able to provide enough financial security if the relationship becomes more serious. In addition, a church staff member's unusual work schedule can make meeting a potential person to date difficult as well. For those single staff members interested in dating, there are a number of important issues to think through, which we will highlight later in the chapter.

What Kind of Person Am I Looking For?

Because of the values and personal and ministry priorities that have shaped the lives of church staff members, most desire to date someone who has some spiritual maturity, which helps them to relate to the ministry challenges the staff member faces, and to be caring of others, not just self-absorbed. By dating, not everyone is looking for an immediate ministry partner, someone who will jump into the thick of things in the specific ministry area the staff member is involved in. But they do want someone with a heart for the church, and for ministry with others, whatever form that takes, given their own gifts and personality. As one female staff member put it, "My standard of dating someone is, 'Would I allow them to volunteer in my ministry?' Not that I would require it, but do they have a strong relationship with the Lord; is it growing?" Some of the women staff members we interviewed found the added challenge of finding someone to date who is comfortable with her being a woman in a ministry leadership role. In some communities, women in ministry leadership are not typical and may not always be accepted. As one woman shared:

> That's probably the most difficult thing when it comes to dating. . . . Is it a reality that I'm going to find somebody that is going to be okay with what I do? Or do a lot of people have the mentality of my family of, "But when you get married you'll quit this job." As if I'm just doing it for fun, as if I didn't work through school for seven years of my life, getting to this point.

Should I Date within the Church? What about within My Ministry Area?

While most of the people we interviewed said that they do not date anyone from within their congregation, this varied a bit by the size of the church. For those in smaller-to medium-size church settings, where most people know each other, there were concerns over gossip about dating relationships and the fallout if a dating relationship did not end well. The most common concern was that the person they dated might leave the church, or friends would be upset as well. Staff members also did not want to gain reputations for "hitting" on anyone, which could make their supervisory relationships with those of the opposite sex more challenging. The risks are just too great for many church staff members, and dating someone within the church seems unwise. Here is what a few shared with us.

> I would say, don't date volunteers, that was just always my rule. I just don't think that's a good route for me. . . . I've had volunteers ask me out and I've had to respectfully decline because I don't want to mix work and personal life like that. So, it happened to me once, and the guy actually left the church and quit altogether. So, I'm like, that's just not cool.

> . . . I did for a short time date someone within my own congregation and I do not recommend that. I wouldn't be legalistic about it. I wouldn't say "God doesn't like it." It wasn't an integrity issue; there wasn't any crossing lines, but the level of discomfort that you can set yourself up for—I just I don't recommend it.

> . . . It's hard to date when you're on staff, right, because you start dating and then they get involved with you, and it's the worst you can do is date your volunteers, right? Don't ever date your volunteers. Because then they jump in and start volunteering and then you break up and then what happens?

Several of the church staff we interviewed work in larger church settings and their ministry area is fairly focused, such as children's ministry, youth ministry, and worship teams. In these larger church settings, they felt some freedom to date other church members but not volunteers or participants within their ministry area. For example, a couple of women who work in children's ministry commented that they would not date any single dads of children in their department. There is just too much potential for awkward situations down the road.

Several staff members commented about the dilemma of whether or not to participate in the singles ministry groups their church sponsored (if there was one). For most, the reaction was not favorable. They see these kinds of ministries attracting people who come simply to meet someone to date, and if they are successful, then they disappear until the relationship doesn't work out, and then they come back again. For women staff members it could be particularly uncomfortable, feeling that they have to defend themselves from the unwanted attention of single men who have come with a strong dating agenda. Here is what one shared.

> [Singles ministry at my church] was very dormant and lacking. . . . Even if it was ramped up and great, that's just not my scene. I just feel singles ministries are like "meat markets." You're so awkward going cause it's like, "Okay, everybody's single here." I don't want to have to ward off people that I'm not interested in. . . . It's just weird, I'm just not really a fan of it.

Others noted that these kinds of ministries for older singles could attract a large number of more socially challenged people, making it a bit awkward for group dynamics. For these and other reasons, most did not see their church singles ministries as an avenue to pursue if they were interested in dating. As one woman reflected:

> Being single in the church is very hard because very few want to put any resources towards it. And, then if you do try to do something, it attracts the more outskirts of people because maybe it's gotten such a bad rap. . . . When I tried, the people I got were very from the outskirts and fringes. So, I think it's hard to find healthy post-college years or early twenties, it's tough to find that just in general in churches.

How Do I Meet People outside the Church?

Most of the staff members we interviewed also talked about how challenging it can be to meet people to date outside of the church. Ministry demands can make for unusual work hours and erratic schedules. Settings outside the church in which other singles gather are limited, and some, like bars, are uncomfortable for many. Many staff members have tried online dating, but it has its own challenges. When do you tell them that you are a pastor or a church staff member? While the men find this a difficult issue to sort out, it seems even more challenging for the women, because of how some men may respond. Using Christian online dating sites, such as Christian Mingle, can also be challenging. Not everyone who uses the site has a vital faith experience or they compmentalize it from their dating behavior. A pastor can seem like a "catch" to some, attracting people who've always wanted to marry a minister. But even here, being a pastor is not always a plus, in terms of attracting the attention of eligible dating partners. A few we spoke with have given up on using online dating sites, preferring to meet people through their friends.

> Well, I had probably three different occasions where I was single and I tried online dating. I used both just general secular ones and then I also used Christian Mingle,

> and there are so many challenges. . . . Do I put the fact that I am a minister in my profile. Do I put that out there? And I tried both. I tried yes and I tried no. I can't recommend either one, but I can tell you it's certainly something unique, because what I found on Christian Mingle is that you are going to attract people who believe they are called to be pastor's wives and there is just a lot of weirdness. . . .
>
> And then there's also the very real present sort of culture that we live in. I met people on Christian Mingle . . . who had no problem compartmentalizing their lives and have said, "Hey I'm with you and I love Jesus and this and this and this, but for instance I want to be sexually active." And you know I would have to respond with, "Well I'm flattered, however there are two things: number one, I am not going to risk my career for you and number two, I teach people about biblical sexuality, I believe in it, I don't want to be a hypocrite, and so there were some non-starters there."

CONGREGATION REACTIONS TO STAFF DATING

As we've said, finding someone to date when you are a church staff member has its challenges, but for many, when they do find someone and begin to date, the challenges have only begun! Life as a church staff member has been described as a "fishbowl," where everything one does is visible and invites comment. Ministry leaders are "public" figures, and we've commented earlier how relationships within the church can become like extended family, with others feeling comfortable getting involved in their lives. Here are some of the complications this can lead to when a staff member dates.

A Desire to Help!

Over and over again, single church staff told us that there were always people in their churches who were eager to set them up with someone they know. We discussed this experience in the previous chapter. Two aspects of this can be difficult for single church staff. For those who are interested in dating, or actively dating, it means that they may have gotten a lot of unsolicited recommendations and advice, and they need to figure out how to respond with grace when it is not really welcomed. Most we talked with recognized that this "help" is largely well intentioned, so they appreciate the thought, but it could sometimes become overwhelming or awkward.

The other aspect that could become frustrating is when the staff member wants help but as time has gone by, people have stopped offering recommendations. One female staff member shared:

> I'm living in this children's ministry bubble world where it's very hard to meet people. So, I'm hoping that somebody would know somebody who they can recommend . . . for me it's been more frustrating at times where, . . . "I guess they

> all think I'm just cool, and I'm okay, and I don't want to get married, so nobody's trying anymore. Or, they think I'm too old and it's not worth it." . . . It's changed over the years, the older I get the more I've felt like, "I guess she's a lost cause."

For those who are older, it may take some effort to remind friends you are still interested in dating and would welcome their recommendations.

"Great Expectations"

Another frustration comes when some members of the congregation seem so eager to see the staff member marry and settle down. As soon as the staff member begins dating someone, the questions begin. "Is she the one?" "When are you going to get engaged?" As one shared:

> It mainly came in the conversations and the questions they asked, "Oh, you're dating—is this the one?" "I don't know, we've been on one or two dates, I'm not entirely sure." So, there was that pressure any time you were in a relationship, it was "When are you going to marry her? How soon is this going to be?"

With apologies to "The Four Spiritual Laws" booklet from decades ago, it seems for single church staff members that "God loves you, and *everyone else* has a wonderful plan for your life!"

Another kind of expectation sometimes felt by women who date male church staff members, particularly pastoral staff, is to measure up to popular expectations of what it means to be a pastor's wife. Playing the piano, hosting dinners, counseling women, being a fulltime homemaker—these are common traditional expectations that may not necessarily fit the women that single male pastors date, so it may be harder for the woman to be welcomed and embraced in the community if she does not fit the mold. Here are a few examples of what we heard.

> Dating was really challenging for us because I had a lot of expectations that I placed on her. And I think our perceptions of what a pastor's wife or pastor's girlfriend looks like, I think it was unfair. . . .
>
> . . . Being in a Chinese church growing up I would see pastor's wives serve, play the organ, bring the pot roast and whatever to the potluck, do all these things, and she's almost like a fulltime homemaker, caregiver, [counselor for] all the women, you know it's almost like it pictures a perfect Christian. . . . I think it's very similar for my wife who grew up in a Korean church and so I think both of us had a very high standards or expectations from what she should even be, like, while we're dating, I think that made it really tough for us.

> I dated a girl who really crumbled under the expectations of dating the youth pastor because she didn't think that she was, like, leadership quality that people could really look up to her. She bought into the lies of all of that.

Becoming the Center of Attention

As illustrated in the quote that opened this chapter, part of the experience of dating as a church staff member is that whoever you date becomes the center of attention at church gatherings and events. Everyone wants to see them, meet them, and know more about them. Your "fishbowl" becomes their "fishbowl," and this can become an uncomfortable experience for those not used to it. One shared her humorous experience.

> I will tell you the first time he came to church. . . . I said, "I hope you understand that everybody will be watching every move you make." And he's like, "No, they won't." and I'm like, "No, no, really." . . . He's not a person who is in ministry, so he didn't have that sort of "fishbowl" experience. And about halfway through the service he was like, "It's like the back of my head is hot from people just staring at me!"

Concerns about One's Reputation

Another challenging aspect of dating as a church staff member is that your reputation in dating impacts how others perceive you in terms of maturity, responsibility, and trustworthiness in relationships. Staff members have to guard their reputation because it can impact how others see them and respond to their leadership in the church. This is true for all dating relationships, but especially true in how dating is handled with someone within the church. As some staff members shared:

> I don't want to be Taylor Swift, and what I mean by that is, you know she famously dates a lot but can't have a committed relationship. . . . I don't want to be seen as somebody that is somehow indecisive.

> . . . There is this reality sort of fishbowl life . . . as [a] single pastor I want people to know that if I am dating, I am doing it deliberately, that I don't date recreationally. Ultimately, I date because one day I would like to be married again. I am not doing it for frivolous companionship.

Also, who a person dates, their own maturity and faith expression, has implications for how church members may evaluate the staff member. If the person the staff member is dating does not share the basic theology of the church, has lifestyle practices in conflict with those encouraged by the church, or is very critical in spirit toward the church, church members will wonder about the faith commitment of the staff member. This can lead to some hard decisions by single church staff members about who to date, or when a dating relationship needs to end. Here is one example we heard.

> How do I date people that maybe haven't given as much thought to living fully for the Lord yet or different places in sanctification—which is not to say I'm

better or anything, it's just that's been my life, that's been the main thing that I've been focused on. . . . I don't want to be a perfectionist jerk in a relationship setting, but there has been a lot of pressure I've felt more so than I think if I was just working in any secular everyday job where there wasn't as much exposure to the public and stuff.

Responding to Gossip

The previous discussion about reputation relates to an experience that some, but not all, dating church staff members mentioned—that is, how their dating lives can become a source of gossip for some less mature members of a church. This can add a lot of tension for the staff member, striving to avoid the gossip, and yet having to respond at times to counter wrong conclusions about their integrity in their relationships. This challenge is illustrated well in these comments.

> I would say gossip has been a big one because I've been single my whole time at [my church], it's allowed this sort of air of gossip. I get absorbed into the gossip and the drama of a ton of young adults running rampant, and so that's been exacerbated by me dating my boyfriend for two years now and now me getting my own place. . . . "Oh, I guess they're living together," or even before that. . . . "Oh, [she] is out of town and her boyfriend is out of town, I wonder what they're up to."
>
> . . . At least for me, being single, any time I'm doing anything out of my schedule, out of my set normal schedule, I feel like there's always some kind of rumor floating around. . . .
>
> They almost always are good-hearted jokes, but it gets annoying when it's the twelfth time someone has made a joke to you about your boyfriend now living with you, and it's like, "Okay, let's all be mature about this."

These kinds of concerns can impact how the staff member feels he or she needs to behave in the dating relationship, out of fear of how others may perceive certain things, and not wanting to fight those battles due to others' conclusions. Here is how one female staff member puts it.

> I will definitely be a lot more cautious. As it starts getting later, I'm the one who's like, "Okay, it's getting past nine o'clock, maybe you should head home now," where he's like, "There's thirty minutes left to the movie, I'm not going to leave just because we're worried about comments. Thirty minutes isn't going to change that. . . ." So, he definitely brings me down when I'm having my "moments." He calms me down, but yeah, there are definitely times when I get a little more anxious than I would normally.

OTHER PRACTICAL ISSUES OF DATING AS A STAFF MEMBER

While figuring out whom to date and how to meet them, and how to manage congregational reactions to your dating are two of the major significant challenges, we have also heard a handful of other issues from the men and women we interviewed and we need to carefully consider these, as well. Each is an important question or complication inherent in dating while on church staff.

When Do I "Bring Them Home to Meet the Folks?"

Everyone who dates has to think through when the right moment has come to bring their date home to "meet Mom and Dad." For some, this does not feel like a big deal, but for others this comes with some major social expectations. Our son was dating someone once who resisted coming to meet us because in her culture this would indicate a seriousness to the relationship that she was not yet comfortable with. For us it would have been no big deal, we had met several others before and would not have concluded that marriage was imminent.

Some single staff members are cautious about when to bring someone they are dating from outside their church to their church "family" setting, because they know the kind of questions it will stir up. As described earlier, some may begin to wonder loudly, "Is this the one?" And even if this is not spoken audibly, the "date" will become the center of much attention and potentially awkward questioning. A couple examples illustrate this well.

> Hey I've been on a couple dates with this girl and we had a "define the relationship" talk, and we are exclusively dating. "Great, when are you guys getting married?" I've been on three dates with her. I got that pressure a lot. . . . It got to the point where I wouldn't say anything to him unless I was like several months in then 'cause I didn't want to have to face that question, "When are you getting married?"

> . . . It was like, "Hey when are you getting married?" and I'm like, "I don't know." There's that pressure . . . anytime a new girl like, "Is this the one?" Even faced that with the congregation too. It really made me think through the way I would post the pictures of me and my "girlfriend" at that time because I knew that I would always face that pressure and that she would face that pressure, if she was in the church.

Should I Bring Them to My Ministry Group?

Bringing someone you are dating to the church is one level of introduction to the congregation. If a staff member oversees a particular area of ministry, then bringing the date into that group invites a yet deeper level of attention and a new set of risks. First, it is likely that personal relationships, with both other ministry leaders and participants, are closer than with people in the broader congregation, so their desire to be involved in the life of the staff member may be even greater. Group members may ask the same kinds of questions, but more candidly and openly, particularly children or youth, who may not understand what is polite to ask and what is not. After all, these people feel the closest to the staff member, so it feels more natural (and acceptable) to be nosey.

Other risks we heard from those we interviewed come very naturally from the new close relationships that may form, as people from the church come to know and appreciate the person the staff member is dating. If all progresses over time, leading to marriage, then all is well. But, if the relationship ends, it can be hard for some in the ministry area to understand, and they may experience the pain of broken relationships, similar to what some parents experience when a daughter's engagement is broken and they really liked the man she was dating, or what siblings may experience when their brother's girlfriend isn't coming around anymore and they enjoyed talking with her. Broken relationships hurt, and it can be hard to explain why things did not work out. One staff member shared a helpful comparison.

> So, bringing somebody around in that sense . . . I can't speak from experience but I would guess that it is similar to being a divorced dad, where you have a kid—at what point do you bring the girlfriend around the kids because there is a potential for them to get attached, and then things don't work out there is a potential for resentment.

How Honest Should I Be about the Struggles of Ministry?

All ministries have their challenges, and we recognize that we do not always handle well all the tensions and challenges of working with others. The stresses and conflicts of ministry can leave us frustrated and looking for someone with whom we can vent. We see this happen very naturally in close friendships and marriage relationships, where space is given to vent and sympathy and encouragement is given to help us figure out how to respond well. Often, as dating relationships form and become closer over time, it can be very natural to want to vent some frustrations with the person we are dating, but this is where the challenge is felt.

Several of those we interviewed expressed concern about wanting to be careful not to "taint" their date's view of the church or of others in leadership. They knew, in their frustration, they could say things that might cause their date to become critical of others at the church, and they did not want to do that. While they desired an open and supportive relationship, they were cautious about how and when it was appropriate to share frustrations with someone they were dating. As one staff member explained:

> And it's hard to be honest, . . . if you meet someone while in ministry. I'd like to be honest . . . about the struggles of the church and that, [but] you don't want to taint someone's view of another staff member or of the church with something you know. . . . In a dating relationship it's really easy to taint someone's view of other staff or even of you on staff. . . . I felt like I had a hard time opening up about what's going on because it was like, I don't want you to think less of our lead pastor because he did something that I didn't like, or made a decision that cut my budget and so I am annoyed.

These are good issues to consider carefully, and it seems wise to not share major frustrations early in a dating relationship. As a relationship grows, and as the staff member sees the level of maturity and grace their date has, they may be able to open up more about the stresses they feel. Learning to do this well, with humility and grace, is important both for the dating relationship and for the same kind of deep sharing done with other close friends or with a marriage partner.

The Impact of Social Media on Dating Relationships

One of the more recent technological developments that has some implications for dating as a church staff member is the growth of the use of social media of all kinds, and the ways in which others can have ready access to a lot of information about us and those we date. Life was not always so.

I am a "boomer." My oldest daughter has observed, "Dad, you were born before computers roamed the earth." It's true. I grew up and did all of my dating before the development and proliferation of personal computers, smartphones, and the Internet. When I was out with friends or dating, the only way others could know what we did or what we liked was if we told them in person, called them on the phone, or if someone who knew us actually saw us and gossiped about us. Today it seems that for some people all of their activities, every meal they've ever had, every show they've watched or silly cat video they've seen are instantly shared for all to see on their social media accounts. What we share can impact others' assessment of us. As one person shared:

> I'm really selective about what I post on my social media. Partly because, like, "if you want to know what's going on in my life, you should ask me and I'll tell you," but partly because I don't need that type of stuff to be circulating all the time.

For single church staff members, who have to be concerned to some degree with how others perceive them as responsible spiritual leaders in the congregation, they have to keep a careful eye on what they share on their own social media, and what is shared by those they date. Like spouses in marriage relationships, the postings of the person being dated has an impact on how others view the staff member. "How can he be seriously dating someone with that kind of attitude?" "How can she date someone who says things like that?" One youth pastor shared this story:

> So, I remember like one girl that I was interested in dating, was a nice girl and we had fun together, but I noticed that on our social media page she would often times post things that I thought would be somewhat inappropriate in a ministry setting. Whether they were pictures, whether they were articles, and things like that, and I lead a pretty public life in term of what stuff goes on here and so it created these awkward moments. On the one hand, I want to let you have your freedom and process through your own walk with God and what you feel like you need to do and I don't want to be some guy that's arbitrarily like judging you all the time. But this actually does impact me, this is my job.

Dating When Ministry Is Hectic and Draining

One other challenge comes with the territory for those serving on church staff is the reality that at times the demands of ministry drain them physically and emotionally, leaving them not in the best of shape for an evening out on a date. Sometimes they just want to go home and crash, binge watch a few episodes of a favorite show, and go to bed early. Dating takes energy, and they want to be engaging and enjoy their time out with their date, not fall asleep halfway through the movie. These examples illustrate this challenge.

> And then just being tired, just physically tiring and mentally and emotionally and spiritually tired from ministry and I feel like the whole rest factor is difficult. . . . Social energy is minimum to put myself out there 'cause that's exhausting going on first dates and you know giving off great first impressions and being on your "A-game." It's just hard in this field.

> We've had a lot of conversations, even in the midst of dating, . . . we really had a lot of hard conversations where she'd say at times, "Sundays I feel a little invisible." And then I would have to say "Well it is kind of my work day. Okay, I will work on making you less invisible but at the same time this is still like one of my work days." And it is a really odd conundrum. We've talked with a lot of different couples about that.

Another challenge is the irregular schedule that church staff have to navigate, with many evenings out in ministry or at meetings, special events, or tied up with emergency counseling phone calls. For married pastoral staff, it is common to hear about someone being a "ministry widow," feeling neglected, like the church needs always come before those of the spouse. The same can be true for those who date, and it can impact those relationships over time.

Though not as major of a challenge as others discussed earlier, canceling a date when an unexpected church need arises can be difficult. Church staff members really don't want to disappoint their date, but it can feel hard to go through with their plans if a legitimate need does come up. To help navigate this issue, it would be a good idea to talk this scenario over with the date at some point, to figure out how to best handle these situations, if or when they come up.

WHAT YOU CAN DO TO NAVIGATE DATING WELL

I'm afraid that, with all I've written earlier, I risk leaving the readers with a sense of defeat—that ministry and dating just cannot go together. This is not true. The good news is, though it can be challenging, dating while on church staff can be a rich and positive experience. Some of our interviewees had many years of experience in vocational ministry while single and had only recently married. For them, dating was at times difficult, but worthwhile and a blessing. Here are some reflections in light of what we heard from them, and from those still dating, that may help you navigate the dating experience well.

Resting Secure in God's Love

It may sound clichéd, but foundational to good dating relationships is having a secure sense of being loved and accepted as you are. With this realization, rooted in the gospel proclamation of God's grace for us shown in Jesus Christ and God's steadfast love for us (see Romans 8), we are able to enter into all other relationships in ways that allow us to love and care for others, not just to seek some security or reassurance for ourselves. Many of those we spoke with really do long to be in a loving relationship with a spouse, yet have learned to be patient and content in this season of life because they trust God's work in their lives. They have built strong friendships with others who are channels for receiving God's love for them and offering it back to these friends. Minus this kind of firm foundation, it can be easier to enter into unhealthy dating relationships that end up hindering or damaging your ministry effectiveness and opportunities. Your ability to love well begins with recognizing that you are well loved.

> For this reason I bow my knees before the Father, from whom every family in heaven and on earth is named, that according to the riches of his glory he may

> grant you to be strengthened with power through his Spirit in your inner being, so that Christ may dwell in your hearts through faith—that you, being rooted and grounded in love, may have strength to comprehend with all the saints what is the breadth and length and height and depth, and to know the love of Christ that surpasses knowledge, that you may be filled with all the fullness of God. (Ephesians 3:14–19, ESV)

Considering Your Options Carefully and Being Intentional

If a church staff member desires to date and is open to the possibility of a future marriage relationship, then it is important not just to assume this will somehow happen on its own or fall into your lap. Be honest and open with God about this, and those you have grown to trust, and look for ways to open your schedule up to new opportunities. You never know where potential connections can be made, and though it feels emotionally risky, getting out and getting to know others and allowing them to know you are important life disciplines to cultivate. Get outside your "church box" and participate in your community. Here are a few ideas gleaned from reflecting on what others shared with us.

- If you are open to recommendations for "blind dates" coming from those who know you well, let them know this, and thank them even when dates don't work out. Trust your friends who know you well to see possibilities you may not be aware of. If they stop making recommendations, remind them that you are still open to any good ideas they may have as time goes by.
- In larger church settings, look for ways to get involved in ministries outside of those you are responsible to lead (more about this later).
- Check out single adult ministries in other churches in your area. Don't let the possible fear of a "meat market" experience stop you from going and getting to know others and enjoying time with them. There will always be a variety of motives for why people attend. Don't let this spoil the opportunity for you.
- Join community groups in your areas of interest—choirs, community orchestras, art classes, hiking or bicycling groups, fitness classes, book clubs, bowling leagues, dance classes, and more. Volunteer at food kitchens, hospitals, schools, Red Cross, Habitat for Humanity—all places where you can help others and meet other caring people. Be active in your community.
- If you live in a rural area, look to participate in activities and groups in other nearby towns and cities. Find one or two you can get involved in on a regular basis, and really enjoy them!

Embracing the Fishbowl

As much as you may wish others were not watching your personal life, as a leader in the church, this just comes with the territory. You are a leader, not just in your "official" ministry role but in your life example. So much of what others will learn from you is by watching your life and seeing the difference your faith makes in your relationships—all kinds of relationships—not just dating. We teach in word and deed, and others do watch and take note. A few people shared some helpful thoughts about this.

> You are in a bubble, I mean especially in youth ministry I've had people, parents tell me "you're the example I'm telling my kids to follow." And there's a huge like honor in that and there is also a huge responsibility that if this relationship ends, even for good reasons, I've got more explaining to do than anyone ever will.
>
> I guess I learned this early on in ministry from my college pastor, that you have to be careful when you're dating as a single man and you're in ministry. I don't remember exactly what he said but he said, "Just be careful of who you're dating, and how much you're dating because you don't want to be dating someone and then the relationship doesn't work and then you move on to the next person. And that doesn't work, and you move on to the next person. Just doesn't look right when you're doing that."
>
> . . . People who are Christians but aren't in the ministry are just shocked that we're not sexually involved, you know, those kinds of things it's also a tremendous responsibility because people are paying attention and watching, and they're a little bit stunned that we're keeping all the boundaries we should be even in our fifties, so, it's a very interesting experience.

Recognizing that you are an example to others can help you respond well to the natural temptations that can come when a relationship is becoming more serious. Welcome this, and look for ways to develop accountability relationships with others you trust so you can model your dating life well (more on this later).

Cautions for Dating within the Church

If you are in a larger ministry setting where you think dating someone within the church may be possible, consider the following issues and practices.

- *Talk it over with others first.* Discuss your interest in dating someone within the church with someone who supervises you or with a mature leader in the church (e.g., other staff, church board member) and listen to their wisdom or concerns. This will go best if others know of your desires and intentions and can help you think through it well before you begin. They may have good reasons to caution you against this, so be open, and listen well.

- *Avoid dating within your "sphere of influence."* Don't date those you minister to or supervise in ministry, whether volunteers, other paid staff under your care, group participants, or parents of children or youth. Don't mix ministry and dating relationships.
- *Proceed slowly, openly, with integrity.* As discussed earlier, your life example speaks loudly to others and it is important to enter carefully into dating relationships with others in the church. Trying to hide a dating relationship will likely not work for long, and it can cause others to distrust you in the future. Be open about what you are doing, take time to explore the relationship at a friendship level first, and then see if it is indeed developing into something of a more serious nature. Remember that you are in the fishbowl, and allow your relationships to help others see the goodness of God's standards for how we love (agape) and care for others.
- *If it doesn't work out.* Most people will date a few different people before they may find the right match for their lifetime. One of the great risks of dating someone in your church is what to do if the relationship does not work out. If a dating relationship proceeds slowly, and it becomes clear that it is not best to continue to pursue it, it may be possible to stop dating and still maintain a healthy relationship as members of the same church. If the relationship has gone deeper, though, then ending it may require some kind of social distancing to allow healthy recovery and engagement in church life. In larger churches, it may be possible to attend different services, or other ministry groups, and not run into each other very often. In smaller churches, this may be more difficult or impossible, and if one of the people involved is not on staff, he or she may naturally feel like leaving the church and going somewhere else, at least for a season. While this is regrettable, it may be the only good solution to an awkward and painful situation. All the more reason to consider carefully before dating anyone within your church.

Bringing a Date from outside to Your Church

If you decide to date someone outside your church setting, the early stages of the dating relationship may be easier, away from the observation and attention of members of your church, but if the relationship grows over time there will come a point when you very naturally will want him or her to join you at some church function. Here are a few ideas to help make this go well.

- *Prepare your date.* You know your congregation, so talk this over with your date to make sure he or she understands how others may react and respond. Just knowing what to expect can reduce some of the felt impact of the introduction.

- *Prepare people at your church to help.* Ask some friends you know well and trust to help you to welcome your friend at the church event and to be available to join you together as a group. Their gift of hospitality can help your friend feel welcomed.
- *Make sure you are available to be "host."* If you are going to be tied up and not available to be with or introduce your date to others, it will not be a good first experience for him or her. Make sure you plan to bring your date when you actually have some freedom to be with and introduce him or her to others. If there are moments when responsibilities keep you from being with your date, be sure you have recruited one of your friends to stay with him or her.
- *Debrief with your date.* When this first experience is over, take time to talk about it together, listen well to your date's perspective and concerns that might come up. Doing this can help you figure out what would be important to do if he or she comes with you again.
- *If things continue . . .* If your relationship continues to flourish, and your date comes to your church more regularly, try to help your date find his or her own place in the church, ministries and activities that fit well with his or her own interests and gifts, not just to tag along with you in your ministry area. The church is intended to be a place for *all* to be able to participate, use their gifts, and receive God's grace through others. If the church is to be a place where your date can grow, then he or she needs that opportunity.

Building Accountability Relationships

Several church staff we interviewed spoke of inviting mature people whom they respected and trusted to ask them questions about their dating relationships. They valued being held accountable for their integrity in their dating by someone who cared about them. Some of these were people who could be very direct in their questions, but it was received well because of the depth of trust and care between them. One example from a female staff member was pretty direct.

> One of the people who trained me, she has taken it upon herself to be my accountability partner. She's close to sixty, married gal with two grown kids, and just randomly she'll ask me, "So, you and your boyfriend having sex?" "No." "Okay, good, because you know you'd get fired," like little things like that. "Okay, good, I'm glad we had this check in."

Consider carefully who you can trust to graciously, yet firmly, be on your accountability team. Discuss this with them and ask if they would be willing to help you in this way. Set up regular times to talk about your dating relationships, and listen carefully to their questions and counsel. Allow them to offer wise counsel and to encourage you to live your faith well in this important relationship.

One other way that accountability partners were helpful for some of women staff members we interviewed was if they were going out with someone new, they would give extensive information about their date and their plans to a close friend as a safety measure. Here is an example of the steps taken by one female staff member:

> Being single requires accountability as much as being married requires accountability. It's been almost been a year since I've actually met somebody for coffee. But I am intentional about sharing with a good friend of mine where I am going, I give her access to my GPS where she sees where I'm at, she knows how long I've been there. And she gets a picture and the name the person that I'm meeting. . . . Nothing is hidden. 'Cause the moment it becomes hidden, it has the capacity, the potential to make a wrong turn and I will not put myself in a position or allow myself to be in the position to where I could make a wrong turn.

QUESTIONS FOR REFLECTION AND DISCUSSION

As we've shared earlier, dating while being on church staff has some unique challenges. Each of the people we interviewed had a different experience, yet they shared so many of the same issues. We offer the following questions to help you reflect on your own situation and desires, and to consider what you might do to better support yourself in your own dating relationships. Again, if you have friends you feel comfortable sharing closely with, these may be good questions to talk about with them.

1. What has been your experience with finding the kind of person you would like to date? If this has been a significant challenge, what has made it so? Was there anything from the chapter that gave you new ideas about how you might address some of these challenges?
2. Given your church situation, do you think dating anyone within your church is a possibility to explore or do you think this would be unwise? Have you had any experience like this in the past? What did you learn from it?
3. Have you tried any online dating services? If so, what was that experience like? If you were to consider trying it (or trying it again), what might you do to try to make it a healthy and helpful experience? Do your friends know you are open to dating and welcome thoughtful recommendations, or do you assume they know this?
4. If you have dated while on church staff, how did people in your church respond? What did you appreciate, and what did you not appreciate? Was there anything in this chapter that might help you navigate these responses better?

5. In your dating relationships, how do you determine what kind of ministry frustrations are okay to share with your date? How have they reacted to this sharing?
6. How intentional are you in pursuing opportunities to get to know others with similar interests, both within your church and in your broader community? If you haven't really done much of this, what opportunities are worth exploring?
7. If you have had a dating relationship while on church staff, and the relationship did not work out, what were some of the challenges you and your date faced after the breakup that impacted you both in your participation in your church? How did you handle these challenges? What can you learn from this experience?
8. Given how important social media has become, how can you manage this to minimize its impact on your dating? Or, how comfortable are you and the person you are dating in knowing that what you post will be seen and evaluated by others who support and/or are impacted by the ministry of the church?
9. Are you comfortable having accountability partners to talk with about your dating relationships and experiences? If you feel you need this kind of accountability partnership, who might you consider inviting to help you in this way?

Ideas for Discussion with Your Ministry Supervisor

1. Each church situation can be different. Given your church context, might dating someone within the congregation be okay to pursue, or would you think it would be better to only date people from outside this church?
2. When a single staff member is dating someone, what can help take the spotlight off of the person they are dating? How can this person be welcomed into the church without being the center of attention?
3. If someone starts gossiping about the single staff member's dating relationships or practices, raising concerns about their integrity, how should we be prepared to respond?
4. To what degree should the single staff member's dating relationships be a topic of discussion with his or her supervisor? What concerns might the supervisor have about the single staff member's dating relationships that are relevant to his or her ministry role? What kind of accountability relationships would be good to develop?

Chapter 4

Financial Challenges for Single Church Staff

> *I want to say on the record, I am not in ministry for the money, but I feel called, and I knew that I was going into it with a deficit in regards to money. . . . The older you get, you have medical bills and you have to save for retirement, and most churches don't have a retirement plan, and you don't have a spouse's income or their retirement to supplement yours when you are ready to retire. So how am I going to live? Because I don't want to do children's ministries when I am eighty years old.*[1]

We started all of our interviews of single church staff members by asking them about their opportunities and joys of ministry, and it was wonderful to hear how much joy they found in the ministries they were involved in. Regardless of their ministry areas, they have a deep sense of satisfaction in leading and serving in their churches. Later, when asked about the challenges they faced in ministry while single, the first things they tended to highlight were issues related to congregational responses to their singleness, difficulties in dating, and biases they faced in seeking staff positions and on the job.

As conversations continued, almost half of the single staff commented on a variety of financial challenges that seemed related to their status as single adults. These conversations revealed a foundational issue worth noting before we get into the specific financial issues of staff members. It all has to do with how churches determine what pay and benefits to offer a staff member. Once we understand the basic tensions involved, it can help us better appreciate what our interviewees shared with us.

ACKNOWLEDGING THE TENSIONS IN DETERMINING STAFF SALARY PACKAGES

Every church board has the responsibility of determining what salary and benefits to offer their paid ministry leaders. This task is challenging for a number of reasons, and while in some denominations there may be general benchmarks to consider for certain staff positions, there is often a tension in sorting out the following four aspects of this decision process:

(1) *Paying according to the nature and extent of the work.* What responsibilities is this person being asked to take on, what might be reasonable pay in our context for this kind of work, and what number of hours is expected each week? How might position title and ordination status impact or reflect this aspect of the salary and benefits offered? It's not uncommon for some churches to reserve "pastor" language for positions with more responsibility and/or for those who are ordained. This, in turn, may have financial implications related to housing allowances, retirement plans, and tax liability, some of which may be mandated by their denomination (denominational standards may apply more to solo and senior pastors than to associate staff members).

(2) *Paying according to the education and experience of the staff member.* What background, skills, knowledge, and experience does this person bring to the job? How might this impact the kind of salary and benefits the church offers? It has been common to assume that someone with more education or experience should receive higher pay than someone just starting out. Again, position title may reflect some differences related to the education and experience of the staff member and have financial implications as well.

(3) *Paying according to the need of the staff member.* This is where churches may feel some additional pressures that other kinds of businesses may not. Church staff members are not just hirelings, but fellow members of the church. As such, more personal considerations may come into play. What is the cost of living in our area? What salary and benefits support does this person need, given his or her life situation and responsibilities? Should this not be considered, but decisions made solely on work responsibility and experience? Should staff members who are married receive more pay than singles due to a perception of their higher living expenses? Does this apply equally to male and female staff members? Should single parents receive more in recognition of their greater family financial responsibilities? Just how much of a role should "need" play in determining salary and benefits?

(4) *Paying according to what the church can afford.* On top of all of this, while church boards may want to be generous in support of their ministry leaders, they also have to work within the financial constraints of their budget. A common problem is that the perceived need for additional ministry staff leadership may be great, but it often runs ahead of a congregation's ability to pay. Budgets have to be balanced, and staff salaries and benefits are often the largest part of the church budget. Good stewardship of the church financial resources is called for, making this whole task harder.

All four aspects tend to be at play in a church board's decisions regarding what to pay their staff members. Paul wrote to Timothy to make sure that the elders of the church should be honored, especially those who preached and taught the congregation (1 Timothy 5:17–18), and churches desire to do this, but it is complicated, messy, and there may not be common agreement on the proper mix of these four aspects. This can easily lead to perceptions of inequity and a sense of frustration for church staff members who find it challenging making ends meet. While church staff may find deep satisfaction in their ministry roles, the financial side of their employment can be a source of puzzlement and irritation. Their concerns fall into two broad categories: (1) the discrepancies they perceive in pay levels and benefits, and (2) the personal impact of their low pay and benefits.

PERCEIVED DISCREPANCIES IN SALARY AND BENEFITS

More than half of those we interviewed did not talk about any financial challenges related to their being single staff members. For those who did, however, the issues varied widely. What follows is an overview of the range of challenges various single staff members faced.

Single Staff Receiving Lower Pay and Benefits Than Married Staff

Several interviewees spoke of the frustration of their being paid less than their married colleagues who had comparable responsibilities and experiences. The only apparent difference seemed to be that their colleagues were married, while they were single. Here are two examples of what single staff have observed:

> I've noted a disparity in pay. Often times, as a single person, there is a perception that you have less need to be paid at the same level.

> . . . I noticed that the pay sometimes is very different if you are single. That's something I'm realizing more and more . . . when they hear that I'm single, it's probably, "Okay, . . . he doesn't have to worry about his family, he doesn't have to worry about taking care of others, maybe we can change the salary for that reason."

When we talked with a few male staff members who had ministry experience while single, but were now married, they verified that once they married they received a bump in pay. However, this was not seen as always applying to women staff members, which seems to reflect a perception that when a couple marries, the male is the primary breadwinner and needs more pay, while the female now has her husband's salary to help her, so a similar bump in pay is not necessary. It is also clear that some cultural perceptions of need impact some church's practices. Both experiences are reflected in these comments:

> I can't tell you how many friends I've had, or even in my own life, when we got married we were treated differently on staff. [we were] financially treated differently, like you make more—I got a pay bump when I got married. (Male staff member)

> Bob was on staff—he was single, but getting married, and they came to John and they said "We should give him a raise." So, Myra's response was, "That is strange. When I got married a few months ago I wasn't given a raise." So, I guess when a man takes on a woman you make more but when a woman takes on a man I guess there is no need. I think people think men are breadwinners and women in ministry are a supplemental income. (Female staff member, names are pseudonyms)

No Health Benefits Provided to Single Staff

In a couple of cases, singles on church staff reported that they did not receive health benefits. For one church, all the singles they had hired in the past were under age twenty-six and thus eligible to still be on their parents' health insurance policies. When they hired an older single staff member, it did not occur to them that this person would need health insurance, but the church added it later when the situation was brought to the attention of the church leaders. In another church, all other staff members were married and their spouses were employed, so they had health insurance policies through their companies. The church staff members were all covered by these policies, and they saw this older single staff member as creating a problem for them. This female staff member explained how this all came about, and its impact on her:

> I didn't have benefits until two years ago. I asked them about it and everyone else was using their spouses' benefits, but I don't have it so I asked, "Can I get a

> stipend towards my benefits?" And they said "No we can't afford it." So, I had to advocate for myself. It was finally approved, and I cried because I was so afraid of getting sick or hurt. One summer I got sick from drinking stream water. I got a parasite. My parents have offered to pay for things like that. I told leadership I can't afford to even get a cold and I can't continue to live in anxiety and fear.
>
> When they hired a single people in the past they were under twenty-six so they stayed on their parent's plan. I don't think they thought through the details. I think with me they just ignored it, and someone actually said, "It would be so much easier if you were married" when we talked about this. It was so hurtful, I had just come off a serious relationship that didn't work out and [was coming to grips with the fact] that I was thirty years old, and I worked so hard to get my masters so I could do full time ministry, so I felt devalued and that I was a burden because I wasn't married. I should not be consoling the business manager because I am not married! That was difficult.

Promotion Paths Easier for Those Who Are Married

In an earlier chapter we talked about the perception that single staff members may not be as stable, mature, and responsible as married staff members. We also shared how this perception can rapidly change once a staff member marries. One result of this kind of perception is that married staff members may more easily be considered for higher levels of leadership within their church structure than their single colleagues, which can lead to higher pay levels for those who are married. If the promotion path is harder for singles, it impacts their financial situations. Here is what one staff member experienced:

> It was weird; I had never been talked to about, "Hey, let's talk next steps for what's your ladder as you promote within the staff—what's your track" until after I was married. When I got married, it was, "Let's talk about when you should become director of a ministry." It was like, now I'm married and I can cross this threshold.

Pay Levels and Benefits Tied to Title and Ordination

As mentioned earlier, a person's ordination status and title can commonly impact pay and benefit levels. In some cases, their denomination clearly spells out benefit levels for ordained clergy. In all cases, those who are ordained can benefit from a decreased tax liability by designating a nontaxable housing allowance and possibly write off some other expenses as well. So, "pastors" may have greater financial benefits than "directors," who in turn may have higher pay than "coordinators." As just mentioned, if the promotion path is more challenging for singles than married staff members, and if pay and benefits are tied to ordination status and position title, then singles may find themselves at an increasing disadvantage as time goes by, seeing their married colleagues advancing faster and receiving higher pay.

> I think I have heard that certain people have certain titles at our church so that they can pay them less. I am an associate pastor, not a pastor, so that they can pay me less, but this other person is generally equal but isn't an associate and they are married . . . they took associate off his title and I wonder if that is because he is married. Do they look at him differently? I have been here three years longer than him and he is eight years younger than me, so I wonder. I don't want to get bitter. If I was married and we needed more money, would they be willing to give me more?

One big difference seen in multiple staff situations is the pay gap between the senior pastor and most or all the associate staff members. In many cases, the difference between these salaries can be quite large. While the associate staff members we spoke with do not begrudge their senior pastor the financial support he or she receives, the difference in their own salary results in a barely livable wage that they wish could be improved.

> I don't know what everyone makes. I am afraid to look at that. I do know pastors' salaries [the denomination mandates it], and it is probably triple what I make.

> At [our church] I was brought in on an interview for a Worship Pastor and worship was an executive position one level higher than me and his salary was six figures and it was double mine. I think it was 120K and I was making 60K. I thought, "One level higher—how do you go that much higher?"

For the staff members who are single mothers, this pay discrepancy can be very problematic, particularly if their children are at home and they are not receiving child support from their ex-husbands.

> As a single mom I had needed more support than I have gotten, I don't have a college degree, no housing allowance, and I don't make it every month. Ministry pays less than what you can get somewhere else, I am a woman and get less, I feel called to be in ministry, but it would be nice if there was a level of support financially, and I am lucky because I [now] have adult kids. I was in a situation I didn't get much child support. It is really hard to work for a church as a single mom and make it.

In addition, in denominations where ordination status may be restricted to male ministry leaders, unless church boards take intentional steps to create more equitable pay structures for their female staff members, a pay and benefits gap can grow, based primarily on gender, even when the ministry responsibilities may be similar.

> There are situations with benefits, like a male director at my level is eligible for the tax benefit but because of my gender I am not because they are seen as pastor in training and I am only a director. My status is based on gender mainly. We have talked about this and how can you legally discriminate against me for my gender? . . . I don't think they even see it. I think if you sat them down and tried to talk to them they may see it, but they don't have it on their radar.

Impact of Gender: Men Paid More?

In general, one area in our culture where some progress has been made is narrowing the historic gap between what men and women are paid for the same work. In principle, we have affirmed that people deserve equal pay for equal work, regardless of gender. As noted earlier, in the church some opportunities may be more available to men than women, but some of the single women we interviewed shared perceptions that, in their church settings, generally men are still paid more than women.

> There is a thought [that] for men they have to support their family.

> I find in ministry . . . in general, that men who are single get paid more than women who are single. The rent costs the same. There have been a lot of struggles that the pay is not equitable.

> I think men get the titles that get more money, that is, men get hired and become the Children's Pastor, but a woman becomes the Children's Director, so she gets paid less. I am not saying every church does this, but I have a sense that in a fulltime role with a different title we get paid differently. One thing that isn't thought of is if you are in fulltime ministry you have to support yourself no matter what your title.

Some Ministries Paid Less for Comparable Work

Finally, some of our staff members noted that in their churches there seemed to be differences in pay that reflected a sense of ministry area hierarchy, with adult ministries being at the top, youth ministries below that, and children's ministries at the bottom. While the staff responsibilities were comparable, pay levels seemed to reflect differences in perception of the importance or value of the ministry area.

> I would not be shocked if I, as the children's pastor, was paid way less than even the student pastor and the adult ministries pastor. That kind of stuff is difficult

> because the reality is you have to survive and have a house over your head, and all that stuff.

In one interview with a single female staff member, she commented that she seemed to have three strikes against her in the area of salary: (1) she was female, (2) she was single, and (3) she worked in children's ministry.

Again, not everyone we interviewed brought up financial issues as one of their challenges in ministry as a single person. But the issues noted earlier are still significant ones that impact some single church staff members.

THE IMPACT OF LOW PAY ON SINGLE CHURCH STAFF

Regardless of the particular reason why a person may receive lower pay, it is helpful to understand the ways in which this reality impacts them in choices they must make and the price they pay for serving on church staff. Lower pay can impact people in different ways, depending on their age and stage of life. Some of the impact is emotional, but they also experience much of it in the hard realities of budgets and future dreams.

Perception of Responsibility and Trust

As much as we may not want it to be true, the pay given to people for their work says something about the value we place on their service. When single staff members are perceived as less stable, mature, and responsible than their married counterparts, and they see those who are married advancing more rapidly on staff and being paid more, it can cause them to wonder about how the church perceives the value of their work, their trustworthiness, and responsibility. One staff member wondered about this after he got married and his pay increased:

> They found a way to bump my pay, like, "Oh hey, yeah we know it's a new season." And part of it's like, "Wow, what a blessing!" That's so nice to think of us in that way, but it's also like immediately, in our culture, money is attached in some way to responsibility and trust and all that, and so they give you a pay bump. And that's happened for my friends, for so many of my friends, or when you have a kid, same thing.

Impact on Housing, Roommate Decisions, and Family Plans

The cost of housing is one of the major expenses facing most people, including single church staff members. Assuming the church is not providing a parsonage (parsonages being a rarity these days), church staff members must find affordable housing in their communities. In many parts of the country, this increasing challenge often leads to the need for both husband and wife to work in order to afford an apartment or house. For single church staff members, they need roommates to do the same.

> It is barely livable. I was talking to someone how there are many levels of pay in Children's Ministries—barely poverty level in California. That is why most people live with roommates or have a double income just to make it. I would love for them to realize this.

Several staff members expressed desires to have their own place but not being able to afford it. Some of the older single staff members felt this desire more keenly than those who were younger. One shared that she finally decided to get her own place, for her emotional health, but the cost was high.

> It is difficult. I pay in rent over half of what I make. I talked to my parents and boyfriend first to see if they thought it was a wise decision. I am a determined person; if I have to, I will make it happen, but I wanted a good sounding board. . . . It is extremely difficult. I have given up other things.

For one single staff member, though she had a desire to adopt a child, she recognized that she could not afford to have her own place on her current salary and so had to place her dream of adoption on hold:

> I can't afford to adopt at this point. I don't know of any adoption agency that would say, "Yeah, it's okay for this child to move into your bedroom with three other roommates." That is the reality that I live in Orange County. I have student loans. I would love to buy a house, but I don't make enough money.

Impact on Dating and Marriage

One of the single men we talked with reflected on how he perceived being in church ministry was affecting both his dating life and future prospects for marriage. The reputation regarding the low pay that pastors receive narrowed the dating pool considerably, particularly in light of the high work demands and unusual work schedule. One of the single men shared his perception of how this impacted his dating opportunities:

> I hear this a lot. Being in ministry, . . . there's not a lot of money in it, you know. And I think often times it's like, the husband, or to potentially be a husband, you want to be the breadwinner or provider in some ways, and so I think the pool is small for people who want to actually marry someone in ministry. A lot of people don't want anything to do with people who do serve because they know

how difficult the lifestyle is, and it's something like a doctor where you're kinda on call all the time, but we make like 10 percent or whatever, right?

Long experience in ministry with low pay can also shape staff member's ideas regarding good marriage candidates, a kind of mirror image to what was shared earlier. One single woman on staff shared how her desires have changed over her years in ministry, due to the financial challenges she experienced:

> I can't imagine being married to someone in ministry because of the income and trying to live in California and wanting to buy a house and not live paycheck to paycheck—the quality of life. And it requires working six days a week and never having a day off with my spouse. I know what it requires. First, I did want to marry someone in ministry, but I had a realization about three to four years ago and actually, now I don't.

Impact on Saving for Retirement

In some church settings, there are limited options regarding saving for retirement, with some churches not having any benefit in this area. If a staff member does want to save for retirement, he or she will need to set up an IRA (Individual Retirement Account). Other churches are large enough, or are part of denominations that have set up 401K retirement savings plans or other retirement funds that staff members can contribute to. However, one staff member's dilemma was that, given how low her salary was and how high the cost of living was, she really couldn't afford to put much of anything into her retirement account. As it was, she could barely make ends meet. Saving for retirement was not feasible, and as she looked ahead, that reality scared her.

Necessity of Working Two Jobs?

Another very practical and difficult issue that some church staff wrestled with was whether or not they would need to take on additional work outside the church to be able to cover their living costs. While they desired to focus their energies on their ministry roles at their churches, the financial challenges they faced necessitated at least occasional ventures into other employment. As one female staff member explained, sometimes she felt like asking her church leaders, "Do you want me to work two jobs?" While working two jobs seems like an unfortunate dilemma for someone already working full time at their church, it becomes a necessity for those serving in part-time staff positions. Unfortunately, the pattern of hiring part-time staff seems to be growing as churches face their own financial challenges and see it as a way to avoid having to offer healthcare and other benefits.

WHAT YOU CAN DO TO IMPROVE YOUR SITUATION

I'm afraid that reviewing all these challenging financial issues and how they impact some single church staff members can leave one feeling very discouraged. Please remember, over half of the people we interviewed did not express any concerns or challenges regarding their financial situations. For those who did, each noted only a few of the things we've talked about, not all of them. Different people face different issues that impact them in diverse ways. Still, it is important to recognize that single church staff members may experience some significant financial challenges along the way. Here are some suggestions for navigating these challenges and steps to take to improve your financial situation.

Trusting God and Keeping Your Eyes on the Prize

Our interviewees made it clear that they pursued vocational ministry with a sense of calling from God and not as their best financial option in life. They are willing to put up with a less materialistic lifestyle as part of their investment in ministry, and they felt the greater rewards in the ministry itself, not in the paycheck. This sense of calling can sustain people through many challenges, but over time, contentment can erode and needs renewal. It can be disheartening when you compare your own lower salary and benefits to someone else on staff, or in other churches nearby, and face financial stresses that become a source of discontentment. While not the sole thing to do in response to this situation, it is important to continue bringing your concerns to God, who has called you into ministry, and to trust God to provide for your needs. God knows we are anxious, at times, and reminds us in the Sermon on the Mount that the Father is fully able to meet our needs:

> Therefore I tell you, do not be anxious about your life, what you will eat or what you will drink, nor about your body, what you will put on. Is not life more than food, and the body more than clothing? Look at the birds of the air: they neither sow nor reap nor gather into barns, and yet your heavenly Father feeds them. Are you not of more value than they? And which of you by being anxious can add a single hour to his span of life? And why are you anxious about clothing? Consider the lilies of the field, how they grow: they neither toil nor spin, yet I tell you, even Solomon in all his glory was not arrayed like one of these. But if God so clothes the grass of the field, which today is alive and tomorrow is thrown into the oven, will he not much more clothe you, O you of little faith? Therefore do not be anxious, saying, "What shall we eat?" or "What shall we drink?" or "What shall we wear?" For the Gentiles seek after all these things, and your heavenly Father knows that you need them all. But seek first the kingdom of God and his righteousness, and all these things will be added to you.

I was married during all my years on church staff, and I do understand what it is like to see how another staff member is being paid more and to feel a sense of unfairness and discouragement. My own discouragement and frustration ran deep, and though I spoke up, nothing changed. It was a difficult time. Try not to let this kind of disappointment take away your joy in ministry or cause you to lose your trust in the God who called you and sustains you.

Know Your Church and Denomination Financial Practices

Some denominations have published standards for how churches should provide for their staff members. In many cases, this is only spelled out for ordained clergy, but it is a good starting point to understand the expectations for pastoral staff care in your church. Even where no published standards are available, denominational staff members may be able to help you understand the range of practices in your denomination, at least within your district.

In nondenominational settings, where congregations operate very independently, it can be helpful to find a tactful way to ask questions about the principles and standards the church leadership follows when determining appropriate compensation for their staff members at different levels. This can feel intimidating to ask, because you don't want to appear ungrateful for what the church provides you, so it may help to talk it over with someone in leadership who you think will not misunderstand your intent and see if they can help you determine how best to do this. Understanding the rationale behind current practice is a starting point for considering how well it addresses the needs of the staff. It also can be a platform for raising new questions that may lead church leaders to consider better practices.

Explore Options During Performance Reviews

Regular performance reviews have many values for church staff members. They create opportunities to affirm strengths, recognize recent growth, and identify areas where improvement is needed. While often uncomfortable, this review process is an important way we grow on the job. In addition, performance reviews can be a time to identify what might be impacting the well-being of the staff member, including his or her financial situation and needs. Wise supervisors make this an important aspect of the review process. If the supervisor is not initiating such reviews, then it may be appropriate for the staff member to ask if a discussion of their financial well-being could be part of the review process. The review can be a natural time to confirm whether or not the salary and benefits are adequate or whether they need adjustment. It can also be a time to discuss opportunities for advancement and how to pursue them, which often leads to higher pay or greater benefits.

Share What You Do—Be Visible

For staff members who are not up on the church platform on a weekly basis, it can be easy for congregation members to have only a vague awareness of what your role is on staff. In many cases, people may wonder what exactly you are being paid to do and not really understand all the work that goes into the responsibilities you carry, possibly leading them to ask, "Are you really worth what we are paying you?" In this kind of a situation, it can be hard to advocate for a needed increase in pay.

Congregational leaders, in particular, need to understand what your role entails and the range of what you are doing to fulfill it. This is not a matter of bragging or calling attention to yourself so that others will praise you. The goal is to make visible what is often invisible in the ministry of the church so they can understand what goes into the job, appreciate the effort it takes, and why this is an important ministry area to support well. The better they understand, the easier it will be to justify that the person in this role is worth supporting well. Take advantage of opportunities to share updates on what is happening in your area of ministry—again, not to call attention to yourself but to raise the value of the ministry in the eyes of the congregation. Help them see the impact it is having in the lives of people in the congregation and community. Help them understand what goes into making this impact possible. Be visible, and make your ministry area visible.

Help Your Supervisor Understand Your Needs

It may be that financial needs arise between performance review times, or those review experiences are not good opportunities to address salary and benefit issues. It is important to work at having a strong, open relationship with your supervisor so you can honestly share your need, including financial ones. Sometimes church leaders are simply not fully aware of how costs in some areas are changing. Rents may have increased recently, the cost of buying a home may have shot up, making it harder to secure affordable housing. If you feel comfortable doing so, prepare a budget sheet that shows what your regular expenses are, and where the financial challenges seem to be. Include retirement planning in your budget, as this is an important, but easy to overlook area. Your supervisor needs a realistic picture of what you are facing so he or she can be your advocate with the appropriate people involved in salary and benefit decisions. One woman shared her decision to do this with her supervisor:

> I was vulnerable with my pastor; I showed him "[Here's] what you pay me and here are my expenses including my school loans. I need you to help me, and understand what is going on, so you see I am not being frivolous."

One hard lesson many staff members have learned is that you must become comfortable being your own advocate. If something is bothering you about your current financial status, take time to explore it with your supervisor. If you do not understand why you receive what you receive, particularly if others doing similar work are being paid more, then find a gracious way to ask. If the answers you receive do not seem just and equitable, ask more questions about the nature of the discrepancy you see, and what it would take for the church leadership to address it. You may not be able to resolve it all, but asking about it can stimulate church leadership to think through these issues more carefully and to eventually work toward a fairer compensation.

Get Budgeting Help and Find Ways to Save

Another practical consideration is to ask your supervisor to recommend someone who could meet with you, go over your budget, and see if there might be any steps you could take to save money and stretch your salary further. Not all of us are strong financial planners or budgeters. There could be some unapparent but simple changes that might free up some funds for areas of greater need. Perhaps your church board members or other staff members know a person in your church, or someone outside, who could be a good, one-time consultant to help you fine-tune your budget and ease some of the financial stress you face. Again, be sure to include retirement planning as part of this discussion. See if a professional can better help you understand your options and feel more in control of your financial situation.

Carefully Consider Supplemental Work If Needed

It may be that you have already explored options with your supervisor and find yourself in a situation where the church cannot increase the financial compensation for your ministry role enough to cover the gap between your income and expenses. In this case, it may be worthwhile to explore part-time work options that could fit in around your ministry schedule. There may be people in your congregation who have or know someone with seasonal needs for additional help (e.g., Christmas sales, annual inventory work), sporadic need for assistance (e.g., tutoring before exams, childcare, house sitting), or some regular part-time work that is very flexible in hours (e.g., house cleaning, computer work from home, editing). But be careful how much you take on, ensuring enough time for rest and renewal. You may find that short-term supplemental work is more manageable than ongoing work but that will depend a lot on the hours you need to work for the church. Whatever you pursue, be sure to discuss it with your ministry supervisor. Then he or she will be aware of what you need to do and can try to be supportive in making your ministry hours flexible where possible. Do your best to make sure the outside work does not negatively impact your primary work at the church.

QUESTIONS FOR REFLECTION AND DISCUSSION

Financial compensation issues are not a problem for all single church staff, but for some it is an important issue. What has your experience been like in this area? In light of what we have explored earlier, consider whether it would be helpful to reflect on or to discuss some of the following questions with a trusted friend or mentor:

1. What is your understanding of how your church leaders decide on salary and benefits for ministry staff? What are some important aspects of this decision process? If you don't understand how this is done, whom might you ask?
2. What concerns do you have, if any, about the compensation you receive for your current ministry leadership role? Is there anyone you feel safe talking this over with? Is this something you feel comfortable discussing with your immediate supervisor?
3. If you do have concerns about your compensation in relation to the cost of living in your area and at your stage of life, how are these concerns showing up in the financial challenges you have faced over the past year? How is this impacting you?
4. If this ever gets frustrating for you, what helps keep your trust in God's provision for you?
5. If you have regular performance reviews, do you have an opportunity to discuss compensation issues at that time? If not, would you feel comfortable asking if this matter could be included in the discussion?
6. What are you doing to help church leaders better understand the work you do in your ministry area? Do you feel they understand the extent of your efforts, or is there a need to help them know more? What could you do to help them be better informed?
7. If you are facing some budget challenges, do you know of anyone with good experience who can review your situation with you and offer budgeting advice?
8. If needed, what options might you have for supplemental work and income that would not create too much stress, or create scheduling challenges, with your ministry responsibilities? If you feel there is a real need for outside work, even if on a short-term basis, would you feel comfortable discussing this with your supervisor?

Ideas for Discussion with Your Ministry Supervisor

1. Knowing that a lot of issues impact how compensation is determined for ministry positions in a church, what is some of the history of how our church approaches this? What are the main issues church leaders seek to attend to in their decisions about staff salary and benefits?
2. What differences are there between the salary and benefits for ordained pastors and nonordained ministry staff? What is the main rationale for this? Has there been any past discussion about addressing some of these same kinds of needs for the nonordained staff?
3. How do titles impact compensation levels in our church? What does it take to move from one level to another?
4. To what degree does the church encourage and support retirement saving for staff? How can a staff member maximize this opportunity?
5. How often are performance reviews carried out for church staff? Would these be good opportunities to review salary and benefit issues?
6. If a staff member is having financial challenges, whom should they talk with at the church to review their situation?
7. If there was a critical financial need, can a staff member take on part-time outside work? If so, what would be the concerns? If outside work is possible, what steps should be taken to make sure it does not have a negative impact on the ministry this person leads?

Chapter 5

Challenges in Hiring and Carrying Out Ministry Assignments

> *When I was single, I'd put in an application, and it had to be so good just on merit to get me beyond. . . . I had to have so much there that I felt like I had to prove who I was and have people backing me more. . . . When I was married, I didn't need as much of that.*[1]

All ministry roles have their joys and their challenges, regardless of one's marital status. The challenges we each face will vary based on a lot of things, some of which relate to the position itself, some to the congregational setting we serve in, and some that grow out of who we are as persons in these ministry roles—our personalities, past experiences, age, gender, and marital status. In chapter 2, we looked at a wide range of issues that come with being single and serving on staff in a "family church" setting. Here, we want to focus more specifically on how age, gender, and marital status intertwine and impact singles' experiences of both pursuing and securing a church staff role, and how people have responded to them in these ministry roles. These challenges are not universal, but we heard many issues repeated enough times in our interviews that they need to be recognized and acknowledged, so that you and your ministry supervisors and mentors can think more carefully about what you can do to navigate them well.

CHALLENGES IN HIRING FOR MINISTRY ROLES WHEN SINGLE

For many singles, both men and women, the challenges begin with finding and securing a ministry leadership role. Because of the high value placed on marriage in our culture and within the church, this has made landing a staff position more complicated for singles. Following are several challenges that we heard from our single staff members as they hunted for church ministry leadership positions.

Job Applications and the Interview Process

Many churches are very clear and upfront about what they are looking for in a church staff member, and this can vary depending on the nature of the role. Many singles found that some of the church staff positions they were interested in applying for specifically stated either a requirement or a preference for someone who is married, and in some cases, married with children. Here is one reflection from one of our interviewees:

> Last year I rejoined my . . . Korean Presbyterian congregation, and honestly, I was not really supposed to join them as a single pastor. One of the rules of that congregation is you have to be a married minister to become ordained, . . . but because I was already ordained from another denomination and transferred I was accepted, but there was some pressure.

In many other cases, though being married was not explicitly stated in the position description, once it was known that the applicant was single there were no call-backs, or if the applicant was in the interview process, it became the sticking point, causing the church to cease considering the person for the position. One staff member shared about one of his interview experiences:

> It would come up in the interview, and someone would ask, in friendly conversation, "Oh, are you married?" I'd say "No." and I wouldn't make it beyond a certain level, for a certain level of responsibility. I couldn't bridge that gap for some folks. Then I would see who got hired and it was always a thirty-year-old with a wife, or a thirty-year-old with a wife and a kid. On paper, we're the same. . . . I would make it farther once [my girlfriend] and I were engaged and were married.

In some cases, current church staff members found that being single prevented them from being considered for a higher role within their church, but as soon as they married, this changed. One youth pastor talked about how this felt when it happened to him.

> It was weird, I had never been talked to about, "Hey, let's talk next steps for what's your ladder as you promote within the staff, what's your track" until after I was married. When I got married, it was, "Let's talk about when you should become director of a ministry." It was like, now I'm married and I can cross this

> threshold. Prior to being married, I would ask when a director role would open up . . . and it was always, "Not right now." As soon as I was married, I was the first one to get asked.

Unfortunately, while job discrimination based on marital status is prohibited in the workplace, it still seems to be an ongoing issue within the church, even when the job description does not explicitly require a married status to carry out the job requirements. In many denominations and some cultural contexts, it is exceedingly rare to find a single person serving as a senior pastor or in roles that focus on preaching or ministry with adults. It is more common to be single in associate staff positions, such as in areas of young adult, youth, children, and family ministry. This creates challenges for those who are single, and it is important that they understand the opportunities available within their denominations and cultural settings. Where possible, they can speak into this to encourage change in perspectives and practices.

Gender and Ministry Roles for Single Women

Many of the women we interviewed had a difficult time sorting out at times whether it was their marital status as singles, or their being women, that contributed to the challenges they faced in securing a ministry leadership position. This is not surprising, given the differences in theology and practice across different denominations. In some settings, women are able to serve in any leadership role in the church, while in others, some leadership positions are restricted to men. However, some of the women we interviewed understood that in particular situations it was clearly their marital status that created some difficulties as they thought about long-term ministry involvement. Here is one example we heard:

> If I wanted to be a youth pastor or if I wanted to be some kind of director, it's assumed, you'll be married. It's always like, "Well, when you get married," it's not like "If you get married." . . . I think people assume, "You're in ministry, so of course you would be married, and like, have that partner, that family unit." . . . I've had some friends who graduated my year and have applied for a junior high pastor role or a high school pastor role, . . . and they've actually been asked in interviews, like, "Oh, are you engaged, are you going to be married?" They're interested in their marital status or their dating status.

Once in a ministry leadership role, the opportunities for growth and moving into other kinds of leadership roles may be quite limited for women, due to the theological and cultural norms of the congregation. While it varies greatly depending on the context, here is one example shared by a female staff member.

> For those who are single, what are the different roles they can play in the church as they age? Because, that's been a reality for me. I'm starting to think through, what am I going to do next? Because I feel like for men [this might be a woman-man thing] for men, as they get older, there are different pastoral roles that they can have, and positions, but for women who are in children's ministries, especially if you are single, what are you going to do later? There's no "next step" or you can be the lead of [the] next campus or whatever. I don't see the guys worry so much about their future as I worry about my future.

Gender and Ministry Roles for Single Men

Not only women find that their marital status and gender can complicate the job search. For example, it may be acceptable for a single man to serve in youth ministry while he is young, but as he ages, his single status can begin to raise new concerns about his motivation for working with youth and his trustworthiness with them. One older single youth pastor reflecting on this shared this perspective:

> [There's] not a lot of fifty-three-year old high school ministry guys out there, and the fact that on top of that I'm single could raise eyebrows. Fortunately, it has not where I am now, but I would not want to have to be job hunting. I would imagine the majority of pastors in America are married, so being single, already there is a question of "Why is this person single?" And then, on top of that, because I'm working with young people, the question of, "Well, why does this guy want to be around teenagers? He's not even married." I think that I am kind of an odd duck, being a fifty-three-year old guy who still is completely passionate about youth ministry.

The same thing can apply for men working in children's ministry, but here it is a bit harder to sort out how much of the concern is related to marital status and age and how much is tied to gender. Many people are just not comfortable with a man working in children's ministry at all. If the man is married and has children, this may reduce some of the concerns, but if he is single it can raise a lot of questions, and any application for a position working with children may simply be dismissed.

Salary Issues Related to Singleness and Gender

Another aspect of the search for a church staff position that can be a two-edged sword is that salaries offered with a position can be tied in some way to marital status. The general pattern in most churches seems to go one of the two ways. On the one hand, if the budget is tight and the salary and benefits they can offer are low, the church may anticipate hiring a single person, thinking that their financial responsibilities may be less and therefore they can live on the low salary offered. This may tip the balance in favor of a single person for some entry-level positions. Two single staff members offered their reflections:

> Being single, serving in a church, it's interesting how when I first applied for this position at our church, it's like they asked me if I'm married or single. Why does it matter whether I'm single or married to perform this task? And I noticed that the pay is sometimes very different if you are single.

> I can imagine churches being more attracted to that [hiring a single person], it seems all around like a cheaper option, you know, if they're going to be paying for healthcare benefits, stuff like that.

On the other hand, singles on church staff may find that the church pays more to others who are married, or offers larger pay raises, even when responsibilities and experience are the same. This can also be complicated by how gender influences expectations. There may be expectations that a married man is the primary breadwinner and therefore his salary needs to be raised when the single male staff member marries or begins having children. By contrast, when a woman staff member marries or has children, she may not receive the same kind of pay raise, due to a perception that with her husband's salary, the need is less. One single female staff member shared her frustrations with the disparity in pay that she saw:

> I've heard that certain people have certain titles at our church so that they can pay them less, like I am associate pastor, not just a pastor so that they can pay me less. Or, it's like, I could have easily had that taken off, and so it's like there's this other person who's married with a kid who generally is equal in our position, [who] doesn't have "associate" in front of their name because they are married. . . . He started a couple of years after me and he came and told me that they just took associate off his name. . . . He's married, so how much of a raise did he get?

We addressed this in more detail in the previous chapter when we discussed financial challenges for single staff members.

Impact of Divorce on Ministry Opportunities

Given the high view of the marriage covenant within the Christian church, it is not surprising that those who are single due to divorce may have a more difficult time securing a church staff position, regardless of the cause of the divorce. This fact varies across denominations, with some being more open to it than others. To some degree, it may also depend on the church staff position, with those in ordained pastoral roles under greater scrutiny in this area than those who serve in ministry director roles. Ordination status can make a difference, and if the church expects ordination as a requirement for the position, then divorce may become a greater barrier. Only a few of those we interviewed were divorced, so we did not hear as much about this as many of the other issues. One divorced youth pastor shared the following two stories:

> There was actually a church in this area, and I knew someone on staff there and I really thought I was going to get in. . . . I was what they were looking for, experienced, they were looking for a pastor to be over their student ministries, and as soon as the divorce was mentioned, that was it.

> One of my really good friends . . . is a pastor with Disciples of Christ. When I was going through this, he said "You may have to come to a denomination like ours [because of your divorce]. . . . There was a season when I was leaving that church that I was just kind of being turned down left and right for ministry positions, and then all of a sudden, I had three offers simultaneously. . . . There's certainly some concerns, it's at the very least a yellow flag that gets raised when people hear, "Why is this person in ministry, and why are they divorced, and what's going on?"

CHALLENGES WITH MINISTRY ASSIGNMENTS WHEN SINGLE

In addition to challenges singles face when interviewing for, and securing, a church staff position, other challenges lay ahead once they assume these vocational ministry roles. Some challenges relate to the particular area of ministry they oversee, and others are broader, impacting them no matter what area of ministry they focus on. Here are several challenges single church staff members shared with us in our focus groups and interviews:

Children's Ministry

As already mentioned earlier, single men serving in children's ministry often find that parents are surprised to see them in this ministry area, and in some cases concerned about why a single man would want to be involved in children's ministry. There have been too many cases in our culture of men sexually abusing children or sharing child pornography online, and the church has not been immune to this. For young single men who love children and want to help them grow in their love for God, there may be layers of distrust that must be patiently addressed over time. Here is one reflection from one of our interviewees:

> I was told to be very particular about what I do, especially on Sundays. If I show up without a name tag, I'm kind of in the background. I'm not out in front because parents see me as, "Who is this guy?" Now it is better because they know me. The first thing I do is I make sure I have a name tag on and it is shown. I've gotten many looks . . . when they drop their kids off the first person they look at is me and the last person they look at is me . . . checking me out. Even with my volunteers that I get to work with, the first thing they may ask me is, "Are you married?" or "Are you in a relationship?" . . . Everyone's very careful around me.

While we might think that single women would not have as many difficulties as men in how congregation members respond to them as they lead children's ministries, they can also have real challenges in earning the respect of parents, particularly when there are child behavior problems that need to be addressed. Some parents perceive unmarried and childless staff members as being unable to understand how to care for or discipline children or as having little to offer parents in instruction or encouragement. This perception can take much time and patience to overcome. As one female staff member shared:

> I've had parents ask me, "Do you have kids?" because we're in the midst of discussing a discipline issue. . . . "Well, do you have kids?" I feel like it's an instant shutdown on any credibility I might have, and any possible conversation, so it's like, "And we're done." I try to counter with, "No, but I've worked with kids at this point up to [how many years of ministry], and hundreds of kids on the weekends. . . ." I feel it is definitely a card that parents can use and it is pretty much a conversation ender a lot of times.

Youth Ministry

In general, it seems to be more acceptable for a church staff member focusing on youth ministry to be single, at least for a while. For women, given the changes taking place in the lives of the female students, having an "older sister" to learn from and talk with may be seen as an asset, especially if the staff member is young and can relate to some of the concerns of the younger generation. In this case, female youth workers may be appreciated as role models and mentors, especially for the female students. This was what one staff member observed:

> I feel like in children's ministries it's more of a, "What motherly experiences do you have?" and then in youth ministries it's, "What kinds of counseling, or

interactions, and talking experiences can you bring to my teenager?" I feel like [it's a] "rearing" versus "peer-relationship" understanding.

On the flip side, there appear to be more concerns for/about men serving in youth ministry while single. If he is young, how will he manage crushes that female students may have for him? Can we trust a young single man not to form inappropriate attachments or relationships as he spends time with youth? If he is engaged or married, he may be seen as more mature and trustworthy. But if he remains single and continues in youth ministry as he gets older, it can lead to new questions in some parents' minds. Somehow, having a married youth pastor just seems safer. Here are a few examples that were shared with us:

> The fact that I was single, it kind of troubled some of the parents. "What if this guy is like a little bit of a predator?"

> There's always a challenge when you are working with people of the opposite gender, but especially as a single guy it's like you have to be even more above reproach in a sense because everyone's potentially a dating prospect in the minds of some people. So, I had a few churches say, "Now we ask this of everyone, but especially in your situation, you're working with these high school girls, is this going to be an issue for you?" No, but that's a bigger concern in some people's minds.

> Communicating with parents and families is important, whether you're single or not. You need to build trust, especially when you're working with kids, you've got to make sure parents know who you are, and invite them to be a part of what's happening, partnering with them in ministry. . . . If there's a guy that's married and he's trying to hang out with your son, I think they'll go, "Oh, okay, he looks like a nice guy. He's married." But if he's single, I think there's maybe some yellow flags, or some red flags that shoot up and they may want to know why you want to hang out with their son. . . . I think, when you're married, you have a little bit of a badge of something, respect or something.

> The biggest thing I've noticed is sometimes a sense that you don't have the same say into families of the church that you might have if you were married and you had kids. I saw this in a very real way when I actually started applying for church jobs a few years ago. . . . I had church after church after church turn me down from being a youth pastor and specifically their main reason was because I wasn't married.

This should not stop a single man from serving in youth ministry, but it does mean he needs to understand others' concerns, where they come from, consider how to earn respect and trust over time, and work to build the accountability relationships that will help reduce these concerns.

Pastoral Ministry

As mentioned earlier, it may be harder for a single person to serve in a pastoral role, particularly if it is an ordained position and/or focuses on preaching and ministry with adults. Different denominational positions on acceptable leadership roles for women in the church can complicate this fact, and so many single women may find that they have two strikes against them when it comes to these areas of ministry. Other areas of leadership may be more "acceptable."

Even for the men, in many people's minds, a married staff member has broader life experience and can relate to a wider range of issues faced by congregation members. He may also be seen as more stable, mature, responsible, and therefore more trustworthy than his single colleague.

> I really, really wanted to be at this church. . . . They didn't explicitly tell me this in the interview process, but it seemed they were looking for someone who had family, who was married, because of stability. They thought that someone who's married, someone who has children, is probably going to be more rooted and so they wouldn't just up and leave after a year or so. . . . It was like, I have the education, the experience, but because I'm not married you won't take me.

Ministry with Marrieds and Parents

Because most single church staff members, both male and female, have limited experience with marital and parenting concerns, they may not be seen as competent to teach or counsel in these areas. If a role involves offering premarital, marital, or family counseling or preaching on these issues, their lack of experience may make it harder for congregation members to trust their input or go to them for help in time of need. Some of the single staff members recognized this limitation to their ministry. Here are two reflections from single pastors:

> Can I teach a class in marriage? Should he be teaching that class or can we bring [in] someone? Or family issues, children and parents, can [I] teach a class in that one? . . . If I'm asked to counsel a woman I think on my part it's important that it's either an open-door interview or someone is there when I'm doing counseling.

> Probably all the married people have the single experience and can give that experience to those who are singles. . . . If you are married, you're more of an "all-rounder," and I feel like they could speak even more into the later on stuff of like dating and engagement and marriage than I could. I am probably limited in my experience and wisdom in what I can probably give.

Others pointed out how both Jesus and Paul were single and yet able to speak to marriage and family issues in their teaching. To what degree must a pastor have the full range of experience represented by those in the congregation? Must he or she know what it is like to be widowed or retired to be able to minister to those who are? This needs more careful reflection in light of the priesthood of all believers and the multiplication of ministry in the congregation.

Ministry with the Opposite Gender

The church expects all church staff, regardless of their marital status, to be above reproach in their relationships with others, particularly with those of the opposite sex. Staff members who are single may be viewed as less mature or stable than other staff who are married, creating a heightened concern in this area. Even more caution will be called for in how they spend time with others and how close their work and ministry relationships become. Several single staff members commented on how this concern impacted their ministry efforts with those of the opposite gender. It also contributed to their decisions to recruit volunteer leaders of the opposite gender for some important aspects of the ministry, to reduce these kinds of concerns and to ensure strong ministry efforts with all participants, regardless of gender. Here are a couple of reflections on these challenges:

> I think it's important to figure out how to disciple women as a single man in ministry. . . . There's a lot of things that make it difficult, you know, the state of our world, our culture that we live in, all sorts of obstacles. I'm not aloof to the fact that by spending a lot of one-on-one time with a woman, feelings can get up and running, wrong messages can be sent in a way that probably won't occur with meetings with people of the same sex . . . but I picture being married making that a lot easier.

> A lot of pastors will only counsel women with a wife, I don't have a wife, so I have to counsel women alone and there's the challenge of understanding the needs of a woman. If I had a woman to counsel with me, when the counselee leaves, I could always turn to a wife and say, "Okay, as a woman, what's your perspective on what you heard?" I don't get that, I've only got my masculine perspective on it.

Workload Expectations

For those who are married and serving on church staff, family tensions can arise regarding how many hours they are away from home. Ministry events can tie up many evenings and weekends, so having time at home with family feels precious. One of the resulting challenges that single church staff members may face is an expectation, or at least a frequent request, that they do more at church events. Whether it is coming in early to help set up, staying late with children or youth who are waiting for parents to come pick them up, or helping with clean up after events, many of the single staff shared this as one aspect of ministry that could be challenging. One single staff member expressed it this way:

> There is an unspoken expectation that because I'm single and I don't have to run out to get carpool, or whatever, I can put in, and I should do more and work more and do these different things. And I think that the allowances that are made for people that are married and have kids and can leave and do carpool, which is great. . . . There are adjustable, really flexible schedules for people with kids, and families, but that's not necessarily true for people who are single. They don't have the flexibility.

There seemed to be an assumption that staff members with family should be allowed to have more time at home, and those who are single need less time at home—even though they have more to do to keep up with chores if they live on their own.

Challenges with Offering Hospitality

Finally, those who are single, whether they lived on their own or with roommates, shared that while they wanted to offer hospitality and invite people over to their homes, it was more challenging because they had no partner to share in the work of preparation and cleanup. They envied their married colleagues who at least had some help from a spouse to host gatherings of ministry volunteers, and they recognized this could be something that would strengthen the fellowship of the group they led. Though not a major concern, it was a felt area of lack or disappointment. One expressed how he wished he could do this more.

> One of the challenges is hospitality, having people over for dinner, having people in for the evening. That's been very difficult because when you're working forty, fifty, sixty hours a week at the church you really don't have time to clean house, do the grocery shopping, prepare a meal, have company over, do all that preparation work. Normally, that's done by the wife, and so there's been very little hospitality on my part, and I think that has served to be disadvantageous to some degree.

WHAT YOU CAN DO TO IMPROVE YOUR SITUATION

A lot of what has been reviewed in this chapter seems outside of the control of the single church staff member. After all, you don't determine your denomination's or culture's perspectives on singles in ministry; you strive to do your best within the context you are in. You follow up on the job openings available, hoping to find ministry opportunities for singles, not just those who are married. You don't control the attitudes of parents whose children or youth are in your care, but you can work at being known and earning respect so their concerns are lessened. And you can and must establish wise patterns in ministry that keep you above reproach and offer opportunities for others to bring their strengths into the ministries you oversee to compensate for your limitations, whatever they may be, addressing ministry needs you-simply were not created to meet. This is true for both married and single staff members. While there is much you cannot control, there are things you can influence over time. Here are several things you might consider pursuing to improve your ministry situation.

Know Your Denomination and Tradition and Temper Your Expectations

One place to begin is to become well aware of the range of ministry roles that churches in your denomination or tradition seem comfortable having single people serve in. This applies to issues of gender as well. Talk with others you respect who have experience serving in churches in your denomination or tradition. Ask for their perspectives on the kinds of staff roles you can expect to see available, and whether there are congregations known for being more welcoming to single staff members. Each church develops its own culture over time, and there may be some variation in what opportunities there are for singles. Investigate and see what you can learn. There may be more opportunities than you are initially aware of.

If you don't see the kinds of ministry opportunities that you are convinced you should be pursuing, and your sense of calling is strong, you may want to have a conversation with friends and mentors about whether you should explore ministry options in a "step-denomination," or other cultural context, one that is similar to your own on core convictions of theology and practice but more welcoming of singles in ministry.

Check Out the "Informal Job Description" Early On

When you explore new ministry opportunities, and find one that seems to be a good fit given your experience, training, and sense of calling, see if you can contact someone from the church who can give you an honest assessment of whether the church would be open to a single person serving in that ministry role. If the answer is a clear no, you can save yourself a lot of wasted time and energy by not pursuing it. If there seems to be some degree of openness to the possibility, you can then determine how best to prepare for the initial reviews and interviews that are so important to the process. This leads to the next point.

Recruit Advocates and Secure Strong References

If there is reason to believe that there may be any concerns about a single person applying for the position, then do all you can to round up strong references and letters of support from respected ministry leaders who can speak to your maturity, stability, responsibility in ministry, integrity, and trustworthiness. Knowing that some people are concerned about the possible immaturity and instability of singles, particularly if they are younger, these kinds of references are critical to begin addressing those concerns immediately in the application process. For those graduating from college or seminary, this is why your volunteer ministry experience and internships are so important, and why references from your ministry supervisors are so valuable as you begin searching for your first fulltime position.

For those who are older and applying for ministry positions with children or youth, similar kinds of references may be critical to address latent concerns some leaders or parents may have. Ignorance breeds fear. As much as you can, you want them to know about the kind of person you are and your integrity in ministry and references from those who have known you for many years and can speak to your exemplary ministry experience are worth their weight in gold.

Reach Out, Be Known, and Earn Respect

One thing we discussed in chapter 2 is worth repeating and emphasizing again here. Once you are on the job, take the initiative to help others get to know you, your passion and calling to ministry, your desire to serve well, and your openness to listen to concerns. Work hard on communicating to those impacted by your ministry so they learn more about you, your approach to ministry, and how you want to connect with them. If you are working with children or youth, take time for gatherings with parents to discuss what's happening in the ministry and listen to their concerns and ideas. Be available early as kids are being dropped off and late as they are being picked up, so you can have informal conversations with parents as opportunities arise. Don't wait for others to reach out to you—invite them to join you for coffee, have a dessert and information evening, send out short video messages—do what you can to be known.

As stated earlier, ignorance breeds fear. Trust will develop the more you help others get to know you. Also, how you handle initial conflicts will be another important way of demonstrating your care for others and your willingness to learn and ask forgiveness if needed. Grow your reputation for integrity and maturity, courage and humility. Be teachable, not just self-protective. Listen and be open to others' ideas. It won't take long to dispel any uneasy fears some may have about entrusting you with ministry responsibility. Over time, they may become your biggest fans!

Be Your Own Advocate

As you spend time getting to know other ministry leaders in your church, and as they get to know you better, be sure to help them understand the kinds of issues you are facing as a single staff member. Don't assume they will know what you are dealing with and ask for help as you need it. Also, if you desire to grow and take on new ministry responsibilities in the church that have typically been overseen by someone who is married, discuss this with your supervisor and let him or her know of your interest. Ask what you might do to become more involved in that ministry area, and what issues might need to be addressed for others to become more comfortable with your involvement there. Explore this over time and see how you can gradually grow into this new area.

Exercise Wisdom in Ministry, Especially with the Other Gender

As we shared earlier, this is an important aspect of ministry for all church staff members, both married and singles. As a single in ministry, it can be especially important, because you may attract some attention because of your perceived availability for a relationship. After all, if you are not engaged or married, you might be perceived as potentially interested in him or her. Misunderstandings can happen as you work closely with others, so take steps to ensure that you don't create situations where inappropriate relationships may grow. This is a good area to discuss with your ministry supervisor and mentors. Discuss the full range of what you do in your ministry role and who you are spending time with, and listen for guidance and wisdom you can glean to establish healthy relational patterns in your ministry area. This will vary a bit depending on your responsibilities, your age, and whom you are working with.

Draw Others into Ministry with You

Every person in a ministry leadership role has certain strengths and limitations to what they can do well. This is true for both married and single staff members alike and is a principal reason for the priesthood of all believers and the value of ministry involvement of all church members. We need each other's gifts and grace, and no one staff member can do it all. We all have limitations, but don't assume that marital status creates insurmountable ones.

While it is true that a single staff member may not have the kind of background to be a strong marriage therapist, just because someone else is married doesn't mean they are qualified either. Some singles have very good counseling abilities that can be applied to a range of situations, not just those they have personally experienced. The point here is not to jump to conclusions based solely on someone's marital status. Having said this, we still all have particular strengths in ministry and need others' support and involvement to fill the gaps and go beyond what we can personally handle well.

We strongly encourage you to invite people with different gifts to join you in ministry teams, using their gifts to strengthen the ministry and multiply its impact. You weren't meant to do it all, and you need others to help your ministry grow. When this is done well, it is your ministry team that becomes known and appreciated, and your own particular limitations, whatever they may be, fade in people's minds because they see the positive impact of the ministry team.

Alternate Hospitality Ideas

Those who are single and living on their own have so much to handle by themselves. The work of cleaning, maintaining, shopping, and entertaining all falls on their shoulders. For others with roommates, it may feel like an imposition to bring guests into the house when you don't know what your roommates will be up to. Many single staff members wish they could do more to offer hospitality because they know it creates settings in which ministry relationships can grow. If this is your desire, don't let your circumstances stop you cold, but consider these following options:

- If you are living on your own, might there be one or two others on your ministry team who would be willing to come over early and help with cleaning and cooking, and stay late to help clean up? Don't be afraid to ask.
- Potluck meals and dessert evenings are simpler and require cleaning only before and after the gathering.
- Invite people to meet for a picnic gathering at a nearby park and you may even have more time for some outdoor activities. Also, since you don't have to prepare your house, the cleanup afterward is simpler.

QUESTIONS FOR REFLECTION AND DISCUSSION

So much of what we have discussed in this chapter depends on the particular ministry setting a person is in. Some singles may face many of the challenges discussed earlier, while for others, only a few apply to their situation. In addition, some of us adapt easily and are fairly accepting of the limitations or challenges we face, while others may feel the negative impact more fully. We encourage you to take some time to carefully consider these questions and see how they might help you develop strategies that may strengthen how you respond to the particular challenges you face.

1. While there may be a bit of variation across your denomination, what seems to be the attitude toward singles in vocational ministry? What kinds of ministry roles seem most open to singles, and which ones seem more difficult to be accepted in if you are single?
2. If you have been turned away from applying for a ministry role because you were single, how did you handle this experience? How is it impacting your attitude toward vocational ministry? Would it help to talk this through with a mentor?
3. Knowing how important strong references and advocates can be for a single person applying for ministry roles, have you recruited enough respected people who can help you in these areas? If not, whom might you approach who knows you well and would be willing to help you?
4. In your ministry role, what are you proactively doing to communicate well with those you serve and to become well known by them? What might you do that would help them grow to know you better, and grow in their respect for you, and your service?
5. Do you feel free to share with your ministry supervisor about the challenges you are feeling in your role? If you haven't done this in a while, and there are some things bothering you, how might you arrange a time to talk it over?
6. In your ministry with people of the other gender, what steps are you taking to keep above reproach both in action and in others' perceptions? This may be a good issue to discuss with your ministry supervisor to see if there are things you should consider doing differently.
7. Knowing that we all have limitations, how are you drawing others into your ministry area who are strong, and have greater experience, in areas where you are weak or limited? What needs in your ministry area might you need help with from others? Who might you discuss this with?
8. As a busy single person in ministry, what simple ways might you find to extend hospitality to others, creating more informal spaces to know others and to be known? If needed, whom might you turn to for help in pursuing these things?

Ideas for Discussion with Your Ministry Supervisor

1. In this church setting, are there any formal or informal expectations or restrictions on the kinds of ministry roles a single person could have? If so, what are they? Are any of them impacted by the gender of the staff member? How firm are these expectations or restrictions?
2. What are the general policies or accepted practices in the church regarding how salary decisions are made for staff members? How does marital status impact these decisions?
3. What policies does the church have regarding hiring someone who is divorced? Are any distinctions made between whether the person sought the divorce or wanted to stay married?
4. What "best practices" should single staff members pursue when ministering with people of the opposite gender? What guidelines would you recommend be followed? What challenges or problems have you seen in the past? How were they resolved?
5. Are there any expectations that single staff members will be more available, or put in more hours at ministry events, because they don't have immediate family members to care for? Do any of the single staff have family they are caring for? If so, how does this impact what is expected of them?

Chapter 6

Loneliness and Supporting Relationships

One thing that is really hard, a lot of times the Big C church forgets about the loneliness single people have. Usually they couch comments in that you are lucky you are alone. "You are so lucky you get to go home by yourself." There are times I am great and times I grieve, and I don't think the church recognizes it.

Loneliness is a huge issue for singles. We live in a world that is coupled. We have made romance out to be the pinnacle of the human experience in society. In the church, we have elevated it to a sacrament in some traditions. In many ways, our world is orchestrated around not being single. We set up tables and rows of chairs to accommodate even numbers and a single occupying a space can be made to feel as if they are throwing everything off. When a single person walks into a room, they pick up on these things. On the outside, we may not see how deeply alone a single person feels in this world. On the inside, a single is often wondering if they are seen or thought of by anyone.

> We wonder if other people see how alone we are. . . . Is it weird that I walked in by myself? Is there something wrong with me? For me I have to do the internal cycle and remind myself of who I am. I don't know where the lie that something is wrong with me comes from, but I need to get it out of my mind. I imagine it would be more difficult for someone who experiences more anxiety in social situations. I will immediately do that internal conversation, "Does everyone see how alone I am?"

> Don't assume that marriage is the answer to loneliness. Not every single person wants to be married, but that doesn't mean they are not lonely. Companionship and relationship don't come just in the form of marriage. So being able to take the call to community seriously and doing life with someone who is a

different marital status—envelop them into your family so there is a sense of community—that is what the church is to be.

It is no one's job to rescue me from my life. I still have to live it. This is my life and I have to figure it out. I have to make use of it—I have to have joy and hope. When you are not mindful of me, then I feel invisible.

Size and Demographics of the Church and Impact on Loneliness

There is a longing inside all of us to be seen, known, and deeply understood by others. While not every married person's experience is exactly the same nor is the single's experience. One factor that contributes to a variation in experience is the size and demographic makeup of the church staff, the congregation, and surrounding community. I (Jane) have had experiences of being the only single person on staff and being on that same church staff where 40 to 50 percent of us were single. It made a difference. Some of the harder memories that I shared throughout this book came when I was the only single on staff. Those were times when I felt alone, different, misunderstood, and left out. As our staff increased and more singles were hired, I actually came to enjoy and loved being single. While the married people left the event to go home with their spouse and children, we headed to someone's house to play games or have a late-night breakfast at Denny's. Our singleness brought us together from different departments across the church staff. We planned weekend getaways to the desert and a cruise to the Bahamas. We were at each other's houses, going out to eat together after services, and even mourning the loss of single staff members who announced they were getting married. Others shared similar stories of how their experience as a single was often dependent on the number of singles on staff, demographics of the church, and the surrounding community. Interestingly enough, even though single male staff members often have more relational connection than single females to other males on staff, that experience can still leave them feeling lonely. One male reflected that at times when you are with other male staff you are made to feel that since you can't fully talk the talk of a married man you don't belong.

I realize and feel as the lone single guy on staff—a sense of loneliness. I can talk with other staff guys, some of my closest brothers, but I know that with their families I am alone in this. I am free from worrying about the things they do, at the same time there have been times we've ended something, and there is just me with time to myself to think. Sometimes it feels like "it is just me."

Sometimes being the only single person is a challenge. When I was at a larger church I was on a team of single people, everyone was single mostly. We were all the same age, we did life together, we went to concerts, we did things on

> weekends together. I transitioned to a smaller church and I was the only single person and everyone was an older married woman or a younger married man—my community was gone. I was lost for a long time.

> I've often had no staff, I'm at church by myself, then home by myself. No one to talk with between Sunday night and Wednesday night and then Wednesday night to Sunday morning. Sometimes that can get to me.

The Weekend and Ministry Event Let Down

The sense of being alone is intensified when a single person leaves the office, finishes weekend services, or goes home after a church event. Older singles often find that many people their age are married. This in and of itself makes it more challenging to connect after work, in the evening, or on the weekends. The most frustrating aspect of this is that it takes planning and coordination to connect with a married person. Married people often feel guilty leaving their spouse or children at home to hang out with a single person. The effort it takes to make this happen can be discouraging to a single person.

> I told a coworker I think sometimes why I get lonely is because I relocated to Washington. I have thirty-eight years of friends in California, but here there [are] a lot of married people and the single people here are in their twenties, so I gravitate to people my age and they are married and have kids and it is trickier to hang out.

> I feel that I have never been part of the club. Ninety percent of the staff are with their spouse or kids. I ask my friends if they want to hang out, but they have more people they are responsible for and it gets tiring—they have to plan ahead and check with their spouse and maybe in five months they can get together. I feel like I am begging people to hangout.

While Sundays are a celebrative time of gathering together to worship and see friends you may have not seen throughout the week, for a single it can be a different experience. Even in the busyness of ministry and preaching and teaching, singles can feel alone. Most of our churches are filled with families and very focused on these families. Singles shared that on Sundays there is a greater opportunity to notice that they are alone. At the end of the day when silence returns to the sanctuary and everyone has gone home, the single feels the greatest sense of loneliness.

> I had good friends, so I never sat alone, but you still feel aware of being alone. Getting up and preaching and sitting down by yourself is a very unique experience. I think when you are brave people don't calculate the cost because you are brave and you aren't falling apart or talking about it so people think it is just fine.

> Sundays were the worst day of the week. They were super lonely. I have talked to other widows and singles and they feel the same way. You go to church and everyone goes home to their family and you go home alone. It's a lonely experience.

> It doesn't matter if I preach a great sermon or how packed the church service was—at the end of the day I am still going home alone.

LIVING SITUATION AND IMPACT ON LONELINESS

A single person's living situation also has an impact on their experience as a single. Some singles spoke of living on their own with no roommates, others with a varying number of roommates and varying relational connection to those roommates, while others spoke of renting a room from a family in the church or living with a family member. Each situation is unique, but the one common sentiment was that when you have supporting relationships at home the degree of loneliness is lessened. Several singles spoke of rooming situations where they don't have a close relationship with their roommate or the relationships are draining in and of themselves.

> I have roommates, but they are not people I am willing to rely on yet, I don't know them that well. If I want to go out to dinner, I am driving through somewhere or I just suck it up and make my own dinner. I have no support in cooking, shopping, and cleaning—it's all me.

> I actually moved out from my roommates and I realized ministry is hard and I couldn't come home to four catty roommates—at the end of the day, I needed space to decompress I am not going to find that support from my roommates who don't get ministry.

For a single person having supporting relationships is vital. A married staff person has someone at home that they talk about their day with, but a single person has to find those people in their life. One single shared an example of being on a mission's trip and rooming with a married staff member. Throughout the trip, he noticed how at the end of each day the married man would call home to his spouse and talk through his day. The single staff member could see how meaningful this time was for this pastor and was amazed at how it was naturally a part of their relationship. A single person recognizes the benefit of having this type of support system, but the challenge is finding them.

> Figuring out who to process with is important—you can't grab a random church goer and you don't want to be venting with your coworker. People who are in paid ministry positions don't always have Christian family support. My mom is a Christian, but she is not really maturing so I can only have superficial spiritual conversations with her—it would be nice to have someone on your trajectory to

talk with. It is frustrating to be in my office and know everyone in here is going through crap, but no one will talk.

Being single, going home there is no support there—you have to call your supporters. If married, your spouse should be your support system. I have to call someone, but sometimes I don't want to have to call and talk to anyone.

When you are married, your core person lives with you. If I have a bad day, my person is in another town, so I have to drive over to them or I go to my family which isn't the most helpful at times. To have a hard day and just want to go home with no support system is hard. I have to reach out to someone to get that support.

When singles don't have someone to process with, they can easily become defeated. It isn't uncommon to leave church after a Sunday morning, midweek program, or event and feel that it didn't quite go as planned. Throw in a few volunteers not showing up, a few complaints from parents, and perhaps an elder who points out that you took a scripture out of context. These things aren't uncommon for staff to encounter on a weekly basis, but for the single staff person with no one right there in real time to share these things with it can be overwhelming. After some time has passed things like this can cause a single person to begin questioning their competency for ministry, which might lead to their confidence being shaken, and morale wavering.

I don't have that person to process with—that is something single people need. Ministry is like being a policeman or fireman and it is hard, stressful, and heartbreaking—you need an outlet.

Even though I am on a large church staff, it can be lonely. I have a boyfriend now, but to not be married can be lonely. I had a long time of being in ministry without having a boyfriend, and I missed not having someone to vent or process with, and having someone as a sounding board. You don't want to do this with your coworkers, it may not be appropriate or healthy for the team. It is healthy to be able to do that with someone, but not in the work environment because of morale. It feels lonely when you are pouring your heart out six days a week, but have no one to share it with.

When you are single and a parent is blowing up on you and you have lots of issues that come up, you have to process that with others, you need someone in your corner to build you up—you have to seek it out when you are single.

Another value that supporting relationships bring to singles is the sense of encouragement and accountability that also comes through relationship. Singles see the value of having someone close to them who can speak the truth in love and give them honest and unfiltered feedback. They hear other pastors talk about the role their spouse plays in their life and they long to have someone they trust speak into the things they do.

> I was listening to Kevin Queen, a senior pastor podcast. He spends Fridays with his wife, and she keeps him balanced. The benefit to have that person to bounce things off of and have that person who says "no" or says "you just blew it." . . . The pastors we have are godly guys—all three of their wives keep them sane and keep them grounded and can tell them "you were a jerk." I need someone in my life to say "you blew it," and I don't have that.

When singles don't have a lot of supporting relationships around them, they can find themselves not being able to share the deeper parts of them. One single shared that they realized an entire week had gone by and they had been in relational isolation. The answer isn't just to be around more people. Many of us are around people all day long, peers we are doing ministry with, perhaps the people we are leading in our church, and volunteers in our ministries. The longing in a singles heart is to be intimately known and understood by others. Those deeper conversations are the ones that provide the greatest amount of support and singles don't naturally experience this from the people around them.

> There was a week when I realized I hadn't had an intimate conversation with anyone. Something happened and I couldn't take it and I called my mom and said "It's all me." Even if someone asked, it would depend on how deep I would go. This support thing has been on my mind all year—I asked my senior pastor "Where is your best friend? Do you have friends in church?" He said, "My best friend isn't in the church." For the married guys they have a wife to process with and I go home, and I have my room and Jesus. I have roommates but it is a different dynamic.

SUPPORTING RELATIONSHIPS OUTSIDE THE CHURCH

Though there is a real desire to have supporting relationships outside the church, it can be challenging to find them. One single shared that many of her friends don't know Jesus, which causes her to be more cautious with what she shares about her work. It is essential for singles to be intentional with maintaining long-term friendships outside of the church. Singles often rely on connections they made in college. It takes work to keep friendships alive, especially with people who you don't see very often.

> Intentional is the word I think of—we have to be intentional with work and maintaining relationships. You may not come home to a support group, you have to find that. That can bring energy or exhaust you. As a single person I have been on the phone with my soul friends I don't get to see them all the time—I have to be intentional to call them so when I have a super hard day, I can call them. It can be encouraging when someone calls you and asks how is it going instead of me always calling them.

> I have several friends in ministry—we went to college together, now we meet once a month for breakfast and share our struggles and talk through them with each other. Two of the guys are married and two of us are not.

> I have two good friends from college and we talk on the phone together at least once a month. These are the guys that support and help me. One of them is in ministry in another state and the other is a school teacher. They have been my support group.

> Friendships from seminary were helpful in being more vulnerable—we could tell each other we did not know what we were doing. A safe place to share frustrations, problems, questions, without being judged.

While many seek supporting relationships outside the church, some find the greatest support in the person they are dating. Naturally, the person you are dating is more easily accessible to you. This is the person you are connecting with on a daily basis whether a quick text, a phone conversation, or in person after work as opposed to a friend who you might connect with here or there. Singles see a noticeable difference in their own health and well-being when it comes to having a consistent person to process with. While this relationship isn't necessarily a long-term stable supporting relationship, it does in many ways mirror the ongoing support that marrieds find in a spouse.

Families in the Church

Supporting relationships outside the church are important, when it comes to finding a safe place to share frustrations and disappointments. Perhaps equally important are supporting relationships in the church for building community and connection. Far too many singles feel left out and alone. Story after story was shared about families who reached out to singles and made them feel a part of their family. In particular, those who find themselves single again due to divorce or being widowed showed great appreciation for the support that families in the church have shown them. One widow reflected on several people in her church who supported her and her children throughout the years.

> After my husband died, many couple friends that we once had didn't know what to do with me. A few couples in particular continued to be my biggest supporter. One couple came out for every important event in my kid's lives even though they lived in a different state. Then when he began pastoring a church in California, he asked me to come on staff—he has been a champion of me using my gifts. I don't live in a category for him that is single, female, widowed. I am a person with gifts that he wanted to partner with and grow the church. He was always mindful and caring when there were hard things going on.
>
> Another family in the church would bring us dinner and hangout with us. When I had to go to tournaments out of town with my kids the wife would go

with me and we would make a trip of it. They were mindful that I was doing life alone and would look for ways to stand with me in some of the gaps.

Another woman in the church became good friends with me and my youngest daughter. She is the most mindful person of me. Like "I am aware that your daughter just got engaged and you are doing that by yourself." That is helpful. Being understood is what we need most in our human experience. You can't rescue me, but you can try to understand my experience. When we feel understood, as humans, it calms some anxiety and we are able to find the bravery, the perseverance, resist self-pity because someone has joined us, someone has understood our experience and that allows us to draw on what we need even if it isn't the picture we would have painted.

Church families play an essential role in the lives of many single staff members. Though singles have extended families, they may not live near them. When single staff members walk into a church service they often feel completely alone.

I have families invite me to sit with them at Easter or Christmas services all the time. In my difficulties at my church, I have the best families in ministry, and they care and are protective of me. It is comforting to think I am not going to church by myself; I am so extroverted I need people to be with me.

Fellow Staff Members

Fellow staff members can also provide support for singles. Some churches are better at this than others. Holidays are a time when many singles are working and unable to travel to be with their immediate family members. At times like these having inclusive staff families who reach out to singles on staff can be very encouraging. However, not all singles experience inclusivity. Several singles described their experiences of inclusion and exclusion and the need for more inclusion.

I have found support on staff, people that are inclusive. At Christmas, I couldn't be with family and our senior pastor's wife called and invited me over for the holidays. It is, "We love you and want to be with you." It isn't the feeling of "We are sad for you." I feel supported by staff and my team.

Over the years, I have had some great, sensitive friends who would invite me to Easter after church. Everyone has family plans. I had some friends who invited me, and it was wonderful, and I felt included and not lonely. Giving people the option to be a part of their gathering is nice and I have appreciated that over the years.

My boss invites me to be with his family a lot. Sometimes I don't want to go because I don't want to be around their children, but I appreciate being invited and being known. I may go sometimes. I don't want him to stop asking because I may want to go. If you say no enough, they will stop asking.

> People want to have community, have fun together. I see these people at work more than anyone else so to have that bond or support would be great. The married people don't invite me for dinner, that isn't a normal thing. I think maybe I have had three invites in my two to three years on staff. It is important for me to see healthy family units or couples who are in ministry striving to serve the Lord. That is valuable for me to be in community with them and not be so sequestered to my peer group. I have a lot to learn from people on staff or in the church that are farther along than I am.

Inclusion in the Church Community

Some of the aloneness that singles experience comes from not finding a place in the church. The sermon or illustrations in the sermon often reference couples and families. Sermon topics are often more geared toward being married. Sometimes the language we use to describe events is exclusive rather than inclusive. Often the adult classes and electives we set up are geared for marrieds. I (Jane) remember the shift I felt after getting married. In my twenties as a single there was one option for me, our flailing singles group. Once I got married, it was like a whole new world opened up for me. A buffet of small groups to choose from, events I could attend with my new spouse, and retreats and conferences I could be a part of. I had finally arrived and there was so much to pick and choose from. Singles in our research reflected similar sentiments about how church life is structured around marrieds.

> Our church isn't designed for singles. There are classes for marrieds at different stages. There is only one multigenerational singles Sunday school class, if you as a single person went to another class you would realize you were in a marrieds class. Life Groups are also categorized by marital status—it is limiting. Being single or a single parent becomes your identity and role.

> People are lonely and want to find connection. The church doesn't seem to value the single person as much in most churches. It isn't high on the senior pastor's list.

> I have noticed [in sermons that] there is a passage and it isn't about marriage, but they will find a lesson from it and application that can point to marriage. I do appreciate that in our sermon preparation brainstorm meetings our senior pastor would ask—how about you singles—how does this apply? He would address it in his message, and he would relate it to married and singles. There is always something that could be said, allowing singles to feel seen and known and not devalued in their stage of life.

> It does feel very lonely—the church is designed for married couples, even in parenting things. They are planning for the man to be the head of the household. What if you are the woman on your own and the head of your household? Even the language they use.

There is certainly a desire to be more integrated into the life of the church rather than isolated into a small segment of church life. Most of the singles we spoke to shared a growing aversion to the traditional singles group in the church. While it is nice to have a place where you can meet people who are similar in life stage to you, it is also nice to have an expanded community with a mixture of singles and marrieds. Not only is there a lot that we can learn from each other, but the focus of mixed groups is much more on community and caring for one another and less about dating and finding a spouse.

> At my church, we have mixed events with dinners and a lot of at home activities. Dinner parties, or after church going to each other's homes, going to concerts together. It is mixed married and single people. It is a mix of staff and congregation members.

> I wonder if it is a mindset shift and we set aside time to ask who are the people that could be on the outskirts. Maybe the young adult, singles or widowed, and because they don't fit in our church that is heavily family oriented let's invite them into our homes, check in with them, make time for them. Set up a routine to do life with them so they feel part of the church.

WHAT YOU CAN DO TO SURROUND YOURSELF WITH SUPPORTING RELATIONSHIPS

Seek Support Inside and Outside of the Church

Though singles appreciate being invited and feeling included by others, it is also good to seek out connections with married people and not wait for the invite. Many times, married people might be hesitant to ask single people to join their family event. They may think a single person wouldn't want to be around a bunch of married people or a house full of kids. When a single person takes the first step to connect with someone who is married, it opens the door for relationships.

> Seek to connect with married people don't wait for them to ask you. Try to connect with them and understand them it is hard to be married in ministry. Care about them; don't stay in your own cave. Make friends with married people, safe married people, and learn to value their experience and then invite them to understand your experience.

> Be more aggressive to invite yourself to things being left out and lonely is worse. I used to be quiet and get sad about it and now I just invite myself along. Don't always wait for the invitation—people don't think about it for a lot of reasons.

> I ask people if I can hang out with them and I say, "Are you just doing a family thing?" and that gives them an out. I hear so often "I didn't think you would want to hang out with us because of the kids." Be more proactive for yourself and what you need.

While many singles don't want to be a part of a singles group, some do and find it helpful to be a part of groups outside their own church. Outside of the church singles are freer to be themselves and share more openly. In many ways a person on staff, even if they aren't the senior pastor, are still seen as a public figure. Being able to connect to a group, or friends outside the church, or other pastors at other churches, provides a better space for singles to receive the support they need. Relationships outside the church play a huge supportive role for singles.

> I have one group of peers, this is where I get renewed. They are guys from the marketplace, people I've known for a very long time. These were the guys in the marketplace who reached out to me when my wife divorced me. My reputation was tarnished, people tend to withdraw as "friends," not really friends. But true friends came alongside me. These are the guys I still meet with—once a month. Feels like a support group, without the agenda of a support group. None of them attend my church.

Find Mentors

Several singles spoke of having a mentoring couple at some point in their journey of singlehood. Some seminaries require single students to pursue someone in their church who will serve as a mentoring couple during their years in seminary. I (Jane) and my husband Gary served as a mentoring couple. Early on in our marriage, we had Thursday night "Survivor Night" at our house. My husband would pick up pasta to go and one of our single staff members had a standing invitation to join us for dinner and to watch the TV show "Survivor." On several occasions she would bring the person she was dating to our weekly dinner. She joined our family on several trips and vacations over the years. We came to look forward to Thursday nights and our late-night chats after the show. She was never a burden to us and I hope that we were a blessing to her. Others spoke of their experiences with mentoring couples.

> I had a couple in my Children's Ministry that was volunteering with me and we had an instant connection. They have a nonprofit called Imprint Kids and they partner with Children's Ministries leaders and pastors and encourage them. So, they wanted to partner with me. When we meet we talk about work and life—it is so life giving. They have been in kids' ministry for years in many

> denominations so they understand the dynamics of ministry. It is such a blessing that I have met them. It is so simple, we meet for coffee, and I bounce ideas off of them and talk about challenges. I meet with both the husband and the wife. Since I meet with a couple, I have seen a husband wife team that has done ministry together and I see a successful marriage that has worked so well after thirty-plus years—it is a great example. The husband brings a lot of practical things in order to put my ideas into action.

> My lifelong friends, three couples in my life that have been great friends—we all support each other. I love that I have people that know me—strengths I have and hard things I struggle with—they can privately pull me aside when they know I am going into a hard place.

While having mentoring couples is important, several singles also spoke of significant men and women who specifically came alongside them as a mentor. I (Jane) think back to so many of my volunteers and even parents in my ministry who served in that role for me. Most of them were older women in the church who spoke into my life and what I was going through, from dating to engagement, from losing a parent to everyday life and ministry struggles. These relationships were very informal. I had a good connection with these women and a lot of admiration and respect for them. It was natural to simply find ways to connect with them and ask questions. To this day, many of them still serve as mentors in my life. Several singles shared about people in their life that make space and time for them and the meaningful impact that they have on them.

> In particular, there is one gal on staff who I feel I have been able to pray with and process things with in my relationship with my boyfriend. The simplicity of her making space and time to sit and listen and ask questions and pray—I never feel like I am going to go in and be given human advice—I am going to have what I am saying and sharing brought to the Lord. That has been helpful. She is married. I have been in these couple of years of post-grad life I have been praying for wise counsel from people who have been doing this and are further along. I try to seek counsel and mentorship—this individual shows what I was praying for she had a heart that was seeking after the Lord and I enjoyed her company so I reached out. I simply asked if we could get coffee and I didn't feel judged, I felt very accepted and like this is someone who is interested in my heart and journey—I didn't feel like I was a project to her.

> It is special when someone who is in their forties and fifties and they have a family, but they can make me feel like their peer, they aren't looking down at me, they can resonate with my struggles.

> I have a couple people in my life who are mentors. Two women that I can be brutally honest with they don't try to fix situation, they hear me out, they don't

> try to get me married next week, they may say "that sucks," they affirm my feelings and they are sorry for me. I appreciate that they are authentic in feeling bad for me. I am a verbal processor it is good for me to have people I can go to. They are an outlet for me.

Some singles find a mentor in their direct supervisor, while others identify other people on staff that they have a natural affinity with and connect with more regularly. It is essential that a single person finds a safe place to talk about life and ministry. Most singles talk about mentors as organic relationships that appear before them. These are the people in their life who notice them, listen to them, genuinely care about them, ask tough questions, and provide support. Some of the things that singles appreciate about these mentors are captured in these quotes.

> He makes sure to relate what we talk about to God. We pray as we start and end. He shows he cares, listens to me, and remembers to pray for me. I come out feeling refreshed—I'm not in this by myself. There is someone walking through this with me.

> My supervisor spends time checking in on a regular basis and can make you feel special in just a minute or two. He is approachable, available, there is always some lesson when he talks with us for being better people. Always encouraging—always looking to help us improve. He doesn't set himself apart from us.

Mentors in our life help us understand ourselves better. They have a way of helping us process our things in our lives while pointing us back to God's story for us. They give us God's perspective on events in our life, pray for us, and support us. Singles need couple mentors, individual mentors, and staff mentors in their lives.

Reach Out to Friends and Family

Finding healthy friends that you can connect with on a regular basis is a challenge worth pursuing. Be intentional about saying, "Let's get together for lunch." Being invited matters and don't wait for others to reach out to you.

> Find healthy friends. That has been one of the things that have saved me I have had wonderful friends who have seen me as a complete person and not a half person and they invited me to things.

> Appreciate those who are available for that role in my life. Requires initiative to seek that out, not wait for someone else to approach you. You fight for it, pursue

> it. Have a group of friends I talk with on the phone, others I meet with once a month. Meet at In-N-Out to meet once a month.
>
> Having regular time with others is important. I have to be very intentional to meet one-on-one with close friends. While friends may come and go in my life I make sure that I have intentional times where it is just the two of us sharing life together.
>
> Use Instagram to connect with others, interact. I'm able to connect more readily with my friends through the use of social media.

Staying connected with family and friends is a way of maintaining a social support system. Many singles have moved away from family to assume ministry roles in their churches. When this happens, time with family has to be more intentional. Consistently making the effort to stay in touch with family and friends who are distant, taking time off to travel home or visit friends along the way are all important aspects of maintaining supportive social systems.

> I drive home to see family whenever I can. I talk to my parents regularly through Facetime, by phone or text. I have to go the extra mile to reach out to people, not waiting for them to reach out to me.
>
> I have friends back home I can meet with for long talks. Friends from college that I stop to see along the way when I take trips. I stop for lunch and we spend a few hours together. I'm blessed to have these opportunities.

Seek Counseling

Several singles spoke of finding support in seeking professional counseling. There are seasons of singleness when you need help sorting out the journey you are on as a single staff person – exploring the internal struggles of singleness, grieving the loss of what you thought life might look like, and battling the feelings of loneliness. Counseling provides a safe place of confidentiality and nonjudgment. Several singles spoke about the benefits of pursuing professional counseling, especially after the loss of a spouse to death or divorce.

> I would immediately get into counseling. You are already uncertain you lost your footing the "we" went to "me." It is safe so you can share things that are vulnerable that can't leave that office to the ears of someone else. Friends have the best of intentions until they don't know how to respond so having that place where you have that one hour where you are sharing your feelings and thoughts and you aren't going to be judged on it. You are going thru the worst thing, so you have somewhere to talk about your feelings.
>
> Professional counseling has helped me come to terms with being single.

> The messaging from the top needs to change. Sometimes you see the church offering counseling to someone who is married, but not to a single. If you need counseling—it's not just for people who are married—it is about you as a person being healthy. "You need spiritual direction? Let's make that happen for you. Whatever you need to get further faster in your personal life and ministry." And it is given to both marrieds and singles on staff.

Create a Supportive Home Environment

A supportive home environment looks different for everyone. Some singles shared that they were extroverts and thrive in an environment where they have several roommates, while others were self-proclaimed introverts who enjoyed living alone. Knowing yourself and what you need most is important in creating a supportive home environment. One single shared about her experience living with a family in the church. As she shared, she got emotional as she described the impact being with a family had on her as a single person.

> I lived with a family for over a year and it meant a lot to me to be included in their day to day family life. Letting me stay in their home, not like a roommate, but like a literal family member. Being in a family unit was huge. I moved out when I was eighteen in Florida and wouldn't go home for summers I stayed at college with roommates. Being on my own for that long it was so nice to be back in a family unit. Family dinners and sharing meals together, quality time and inclusion with dinners, trips, doing life together as if I was their child. I was a part of their family. We would do day trips, like to San Diego, beach, or a hike—it was real quality time.

> I loved living with a family in our church. We would all debrief after work every day, sharing in the highs and lows, venting about frustrations and everything in between. They would know when I had a big meeting at work—when my family was coming into town. They would open their home to my family too. They became my family here.

Some have found living with roommates to be financially more feasible, but emotionally more challenging. There are challenges that come with having roommates. Some describe roommates as another ministry to come home to, while others find greater support and encouragement in these relationships. Singles often talk about the revolving door of roommates and the difficulty of watching roommate after roommate getting married. Some try living with coworkers and find that work becomes all encompassing. Some find a house full of people life giving and others call it draining. Experiences with roommates, as well as whether or not to have a roommate, varied among the singles we interviewed. Here are just a few of the comments we heard.

> I felt like I was pouring my heart out in ministry six days a week, I needed to feel like I had a home where it was a sanctuary a place I could come home and rest and with roommates it wasn't that. With my coworker it was hard to turn off work, we would always talk about work. I couldn't escape work then.
>
> It is a necessity financially. I couldn't afford to live on my own. I am lucky my roommate is my friend. My biggest fear as we move into a new place is that she will date someone and get married in a couple of years and here I am again moving again and finding the next roommate. I need a roommate relationally and financially.
>
> I have moved eleven times in four years, and I think out of the eleven moves six of them were because people got married. So, the weight of where I move next, I may have to move again. I never am going to be established because I don't have someone to do it with permanently. I don't have a spouse or kids to go home so the weight of people not understanding that I have a lot of relationships that I am working out and through when I go home. One of my roommates this year went through a mental illness and that has been heartbreaking and hard to navigate. I think those that are married don't think I have to work on relationships like they do in their marriage, but I have had a heavy season in that.

While there is no right living situation, knowing yourself, your tendencies, and what will be the healthiest situation for you is vitally important. One single male expressed his appreciation for having people around at the end of the day. Roommates provide someone to talk to, have dinner with, and watch television. They also provide some natural accountability in dating relationships, potential addictions, and the use of technology. Others find that having a quiet place to return after work is much more life giving to them than shared space as seen in this comment.

> Days in ministry can be long and draining. I have a long drive home so coming home to who ate whose leftovers, or one of them having friends over, or coming home to them and their boyfriend making out on couch. I am on the line of extroverted to introverted it varies day to day but usually after a long day I need alone time. So, sharing a room with someone didn't work, there was someone in living room and bedroom. Even if you put in your earphones, they still talk to you. I was spending a lot of money going to cafes and movies to be alone, so I reallocated the money to paying more rent and having my own place. It is a lot healthier for me.

It is imperative that singles find what works for them and create a healthy living environment for themselves. Whether living on your own, renting a room from a family, living with your own family, or having roommates, find what will be most life giving to you. Homes that become havens allow for singles to find the rest and renewal they need for ministry.

While going it alone as a single in ministry can be lonely, singles find that surrounding themselves with a myriad of supporting relationships is what is most helpful. It can be challenging to put yourself out there, work at maintaining relationships, and ask for help, but those who do find incredible support. Be proactive in seeking support inside and outside the church, look for others who can serve as mentors, consistently reach out to friends and family in your life, seek professional counseling, and create a supportive home environment for yourself.

Singles as well as marrieds need to do life and ministry in community with others.

QUESTIONS FOR REFLECTION AND DISCUSSION

It is evident that despite the fact that ministry is about being with people a single person can feel the depths of loneliness in the midst of ministry. The questions that follow are designed to help you think through your own experiences and surface ideas that might help you create supporting relationships that sustain you in ministry. We would encourage you to find a close friend or colleague who you feel comfortable sharing with, as these may be good questions to discuss together.

1. Take some time to think about your own experience as a single on staff. What is the demographic makeup of your church staff, your congregation, and your community? What impact does that have on you?
2. Who are your supporting relationships both inside and outside of the church? In what ways do you need to create more supporting relationships? In what ways do you need to strengthen your existing supporting relationships? How might you go about doing so?
3. What families in your church are you most drawn to or seem to be most drawn to you? How might you reach out to these families and let them know that you would like to be more of a part of them?
4. What are Sundays like for you? How can you more strategically plan your Sundays to sit with others in the main service and plan lunch with someone after the service? What is the best way to rejuvenate your soul on Sunday and guard against the loneliness that Sundays sometimes bring?
5. In what ways is your current living situation giving you life? In what ways is it draining you? Is there anything in your living situation that needs to be changed in order to create a more healthy living environment for you?

6. Who are the people in your life that you can rely on? Who can you process with, call if you need help, and rely on to be there for you? Who can you bounce things off of and ask for their feedback? Who in your life will speak the truth in love and hold you accountable?
7. Who are your mentors? Are there older singles you could reach out to as mentors? Are there individuals or couples that might be good mentors for you? What could you do to make a connection with them more regularly?

Ideas for Discussion with Your Ministry Supervisor

1. What is your experience as a single person in our church? In what ways could we be more sensitive and inclusive for you, other singles on staff, and singles in our church?
2. In what ways do you feel alone in life and in ministry? What might we do differently as a church to support you better in these things?
3. In what ways might I support you better? In what ways might our church staff and congregation support you better?
4. What is it like for you when you go home after work or after a weekend of ministry? What is your current living situation and in what ways might we help you create a healthy living environment?
5. How might our church integrate singles more into the life of the church? What groups in our church might feel left out (e.g., young adults, single parents, widows, elderly)?

Chapter 7

Building Healthy Staff Relationships

My church staff have all come alongside me in one way or another, whether to help with an event I am putting on, or let me bounce ideas off them, or have me over for dinner every week. They are my extended family.

In many ways, a church staff is like a family, and depending on the size of the family relationships will vary. Those on a small church staff may find themselves the only single person on staff, while those on a larger church staff often find great comradery with other singles on staff. Interestingly enough, not all singles have the same relational experience on staff. In fact, there are some stark differences when it comes to gender and building healthy staff relationships.

Single male staff seem to have less roadblocks when it comes to establishing strong relationships with senior church leaders. This is probably due to the fact that most of our senior leaders are male. My (Jane) experience has been that single male staff are actually sought out by senior church leaders as people to invest in and mentor. My senior leader often met with single male staff members individually and in groups, traveled with them to conferences, and invited them to accompany him when he was traveling nationally or internationally. Single male staff members often had more access to our senior leader than other staff did, especially more than single female staff members.

Though single male staff seem to have an easier time building relationships with male superiors and colleagues, they do face challenges when interacting with females on staff. Single males described greater hesitation when meeting with both single and married female colleagues. As one male shared, "A lot of one-on-one time with a woman can stir feelings." Another single male mentioned the challenge it can be to navigate working with single females on staff who you may or may not be attracted to and at the same time you must also navigate the appropriate boundary of working with female staff members who are married. Either way single male staff acknowledge that they are more aware of the need to set friendship boundaries as they relate to the opposite gender. They are ever mindful that they don't want to let themselves go down a road of leading someone on or developing an attraction for a woman who is married. Some respond to this dilemma by being guarded in their relationships with the opposite gender or simply avoiding any relationship altogether.

Female staff members have their own unique challenges in building healthy staff relationships. A few female staff members mentioned the late Reverend Billy Graham who early on in his career established what has come to be known as the "Billy Graham Rule." As a young man, Reverend Graham held a conference with a small number of Christian associates and each of them came up with a list of problems in the evangelical community as well as ways to address the problems. High on the list was sexual immorality among some preachers who were often traveling for extended periods away from their families. The men pledged to avoid situations that may appear suspicious in order to remain above reproach. This pledge became known as the Billy Graham Rule and from that day on he did not travel, meet or eat alone with a woman other than his wife. Other Christian leaders, including Vice President Mike Pence, have followed suit in adhering to their own version of limiting the types of interactions they have with female staff members.

Though female staff members can appreciate the desire pastors have to guard themselves against any form of immorality or accusation of impropriety, they also desire to have the same opportunities and access to mentoring that they see single males experiencing. Single female staff members often feel that male pastors treat them more cautiously. Younger single female staff members can inadvertently be made to feel that they are more dangerous to be around. This dynamic is always at play even if not explicitly expressed, and after a while, it begins to erode staff relationships. Single female staff members may experience a feeling of physical and emotional distance when relating to male staff members. This can be very frustrating for single female staff members as expressed by the following comments.

> I think single women, especially if single and younger, are treated more cautiously, more protectively, and sometimes like they are more dangerous. A simple example: so couples who are willing to invite a single over for dinner typically find it easier to invite a single man rather than a single female. There is that fear that we are all seductresses. I think it is harder for single women than men. It is already harder for women in ministry and being single adds another layer of challenge.

> I don't appreciate the whole Billy Graham Rule—that is an obstacle. Just because I am single doesn't mean I want to have an affair with someone's husband. I would happily sign a statement that I don't want to have an affair, but I also don't want to be declined the same opportunities as my male or married counterparts, like being invited to lunch.

> Because I am a single female, I think there are more boundaries than if I was a married woman. They would never ride in a car, a man and a woman, or be in an office with a closed door, but I feel there would be less tension if I was married. But I am a single woman so sometimes I feel like a Jezebel and dirty like something is going to happen. There is an extra boundary and they are not in any danger.

Sadly, single female staff members are often kept at a distance and are made to feel like a threat to men on staff. Female staff members share stories of not being invited out to lunch with male colleagues or included in dinner parties. While this may seem like a subtle exclusion of women, even inadvertent and unintentional, other situations are more overt. One female staff member shared of her experience around a pastoral retreat that was being planned without her knowledge. At the end of a staff meeting, she heard two male staff members say, "Are we going to room together dude?" This caught her off guard since she hadn't heard anything about an upcoming staff retreat. She decided as hard as it was she needed to talk to her supervisor who was the executive pastor.

> So, I went to my supervisor and asked what is going on? He said yes, we are going on a pastor's retreat and you can't go because it is a group of men. He said you can't go because of the housing situation—you are the only girl.

The hurt was overwhelming as she recounted the feelings that came up for her during this time. The pastor did allow her to take her own three-day retreat at home while they were away in the mountains as a staff, but the disappointment and frustration of being left behind and overlooked still gnawed at her spirit. The ultimate test of her emotions came on Sunday morning as the male staff members prepared to leave for the retreat just outside her office.

> They were all leaving on Sunday after church and they all parked right by my office window, so there I sat watching them all leave together. I was tired; I was screaming inside and couldn't wait to get out of there. All the while, I smiled. I thought, "How are none of these guys caring about me?" I thought if I walk out with my attitude then they may say something, and I may just say something I would regret—so I sat in my office and just waited for them to leave. I just got more frustrated and then I left. I did cry over it.

She went on to describe to me that her supervisor had given her a copy of all the retreat materials they would be covering so she could go through it on her own. The next morning alone in her apartment she began going over the materials, but her spirit that morning was greatly disturbed and hurt.

> I spent two to three hours just with worship music playing and talking to God at my house. I had to set aside my anger and bitterness that I got left behind and disregarded. The worst part was that they didn't seem to even address this and none of them thought of me in this, only the Spanish pastor reached out prior to the retreat and said, "This isn't right, and I will be praying for you over this retreat." Even when they all came back my boss stopped by and asked me how my time was, and I told him, "The one thing that is bugging me is that you all packed up right outside my window and it hurt my feelings so bad." He said, "I don't want to make an excuse, but we are just a group of dumb guys and we didn't realize." The senior pastor never apologized or ever talked to me about it.

A single male staff member would have had the opportunity to attend the retreat; however, the single female staff member did not. This situation highlights the hurt and frustration that single female staff members often encounter in the church—the sense of being left out, undervalued, or dismissed. Being the first female on staff may have played into this situation. It was evident that no one thought this thoroughly through. In this case the single female staff member was so overwhelmed with emotion that though she thought of potential solutions like driving in a separate car, having another female at the retreat, or getting a hotel room that was separate from the cabin, it was difficult for her to express these things to her supervisor.

> I feel the biggest issue was male versus female and they didn't seem to want to work around solutions. Moving forward that will change. But, it was a poor start to our new launch of our mission. It made me feel not worthy, cared about, or valued. It wasn't just about the retreat, that incident led into a time period where I asked myself, "Am I valued here? Are they going to care for me as a person? Do I want to deal with this? Can I accept this? Now that they have a female pastor will they change?"

Single female staff members share freely about the challenge of connecting socially with male staff members. They described watching male staff members go out to lunch with each other and hang out after work or on the weekends together. Couples on staff have each other over for dinner or do things together after church. These types of social interactions create informal times of connection and relationship building. To those of us who are part of the married group missing out on going to a dinner party with other staff members and their families might not seem like a big deal. To a single person on staff, especially a single female who is on a predominately male staff, it can leave them feeling very isolated or simply wondering where they fit in.

> I miss out on relationships. I am relationally driven, and by not being invited I miss out on the bonding that takes place. I think they are missing out as well; they are not getting my perspective and not getting to know me outside of the walls of the church. I would be more free-spirited if I was out doing an activity. They would see the human side of me, the person. When I feel isolated, it is not good for me or my morale.

> We have a pretty large staff and anytime you get to spend with senior leadership in work setting or outside of work setting is rare. To watch people who are married get more time with senior leadership because they're married is frustrating. Because you want them to know you deeply and in a way that affects the way they think about you in a work setting. So, if there was anything brought to leadership about your ministry area there is the thought that you don't know me well enough to advocate for me to a parent. Or you don't know my heart well enough to know why I am passionate about junior highers.

> Sometimes our head pastor will do a pastor and wives dinner and I don't typically get invited because it is mostly couples. There is even a struggle that pastors wives get together and do stuff together. Obviously, I am not a wife of a pastor, but I am a pastor so how do I fit into a group? We are not hanging out with pastors' wives and it looks different to not be the pastor's wife, but to be the pastor.

Since people are naturally drawn to people who are like them both single male and female staff members may even find it difficult to connect with same gender staff members who are married. Staff members who are married tend to get together with other married couples on staff and have each other over for dinner or game nights. Staff members with young children hang out at the beach together with other staff members who also have young children. You might see staff members even vacationing together with each other. Most of these types of relational gatherings exclude anyone who is single on staff. This often leaves the single person on staff feeling even more left out. For many it is also a reminder of what others their age have that they don't yet have, but long to have.

> There are a few staff members who are younger with kids and they do life together. They have toddlers running around and go to the beach or vacations together. It can feel like I miss out on that because that is what I want. I wanted a solid community of strong Christian friends with kids the same age and be able to travel with them. I think it is a little bit of fear of what others are doing because they are at the stage of life.

> My new boss, I love her, but she is more connected to one of my staff members and her family because they have kids the same ages and I feel left out. I actually

> connect better with my supervisor than my staff member does, but I don't get invited to spend time with her outside the office because I don't have kids.

Beyond connection and relationship building is the natural sharing of information that happens during informal times together. A good friend of mine shared that she felt at an information disadvantage because she wasn't invited over to the senior leader's house for hot tub night. Evidently this was where the "meeting after the meeting" took place. I know she wouldn't have wanted to be invited to hot tub night, but this was representative of many times that she felt left out of conversations, not able to weigh in on decisions, or simply missed out on gaining more information because she was excluded from after-hour hangouts. These informal connection points also create greater opportunities for sharing our heart and passion, as well as hearing the heart and passion of others. In the context of daily office interactions and busy ministry schedules, we often don't have time to connect more deeply. One single staff member described the benefit of deeper connections.

> When you spend time with others outside the office, you learn more about them and their heart and passion. If they knew my heart, it might help them trust my decision making or if I knew their heart it might help me even trust their decision making. Spending more time with them outside of work allows us to understand their heart and why they make their decisions. I don't get to see this because I don't get that time with them.

In particular, single female staff members feel that they have to work harder than single men to have their voice heard. It appears to them that somehow their experience doesn't have the breadth or doesn't warrant the respect that their male counterparts receive. Some of this may be the result of not being mentored or developed in the same way as single men or lacking the opportunities to have regular interactions with senior leaders.

Single female staff members also face their own challenges when supervising and supporting male colleagues and males in their ministries. One female leader spoke about an experience she had while supervising a male on staff. The male was a strong leader in his own right and in the course of meeting one-on-one together she noticed that he started having strong reactions to her. As this continued to evidence itself, she eventually spoke to her supervisor about it. She went on to say:

> My supervisor came to me and said, "I am going to say something to you that may seem awkward, but you need to understand it. As much as we don't want sexuality to be a part of this, we can't separate it. You are an attractive single woman who is his supervisor and you have some power over him, and his marriage is struggling, and he has no idea how to relate to you and he can't know

those things are happening inside of himself. This is why he is reacting." This was very eye-opening to me, I didn't want that to be the reality, but it was.

While there are good reasons for being mindful in how we build relationships with the opposite gender, there is much agreement on the value of building healthy relationships. Though single female staff members often feel dismissed, left out, or distanced from male staff members, they also have a great appreciation for males on staff who are intentional about connecting with them. Single males often feel that they have to be cautious and careful in their interactions with female staff members. While they also appreciate relational connections, they also may not need or desire the same level of connection that female staff members do. The following will describe several ideas for building healthy relationships among single and married staff members, both men and women.

IDEAS FOR BUILDING HEALTHY RELATIONSHIPS

Set Up One-on-One Meetings

I (Jane) recently spoke to a single female undergraduate student who was interning at a large church. As she shared about her experience she kept mentioning that even though she was interning under the high school pastor she was assigned to meet one-on-one with the female associate pastor. This type of story plays out over and over again in churches where female staff members are relegated to meeting one-on-one with other females on staff while male staff members have the advantage of being mentored by senior organizational leaders. While there was much that this intern could learn from the female associate pastor, the high school pastor had more years of ministry experience, greater exposure to more aspects of the overall church ministry, and a graduate degree in spiritual formation. When this occurs, female staff members lose out on valuable interactions with senior leaders.

One of the greatest pathways to being developed is through one-on-one meetings with other leaders. Having a weekly one-on-one with a supervisor gives singles an opportunity to talk through ministry assignments, seek clarity and guidance, debrief and review, and receive personal and professional accountability. Many leaders struggle with setting and keeping consistent one-on-one meetings with their people. It is far too easy to cancel and reschedule these times, which is why it is crucial that singles express the importance that this connection point is for them. It takes great time, commitment, and discipline to make regular one-on-one meetings a priority. The lack of meetings can certainly cause a drift in alignment and disconnection among staff members. Since singles often feel alone in ministry, having regular one-on-ones with a ministry leader provides great support. Whether weekly, bimonthly, or monthly, pursuing consistent connection with supervisors will be time well spent.

While both singles and marrieds benefit from one-on-ones, singles in particular appreciate the personal connection and accountability that one-on-ones provide. The following are possible topics to explore with your supervisor:

- How am I doing with work and life balance?
- What does my community outside of the church look like?
- How connected am I feeling inside the church?
- Am I having opportunities to spend time with my immediate family?
- How might I get more involved in the larger church community?
- In what ways do I need greater support from my supervisor and others on staff?

Several singles spoke of senior leaders who mentored and supported them by meeting with them regularly. It is so beneficial to have consistent one-on-ones to address work and personal issues. Singles appreciate when senior leaders are willing to engage all aspects of their life acknowledging their singleness and some of the additional support they might need because of it, all the while not treating them differently because of their singleness or trying to fix them.

> Our senior pastor is a huge support. We have a standing meeting on Thursdays. I appreciate that he has never made a distinction because I am single. He has never made a comment about it or tried to set me up. I told him thank you for that recently. He wants our church to be a place where singles feel welcomed. He has subtle ways of making them have a part. He is a huge support.

> When I came to my church, the executive pastor asked me, "How can the church support you as a single person?" I had never been asked that by any other person at a church. I think that is something to consider how can the church come alongside me as a single person. He said, "We don't want you to feel you aren't valued."

While relationships with senior leaders are important, they aren't the only relationships that make a difference for a single person. I (Jane) made every effort in my twenties as a single person on staff to seek out opportunities to meet with others on staff. Sometimes this meant taking my female associate to off-campus meetings with me if I was meeting with a male staff member or simply taking the time to drop by the office of another staff member to make a quick connection. Creating space to connect and going out of my way to take the first step toward that connection allowed me a sounding board for my thoughts and ideas and relational connections that served me well as I navigated ministry life. I found that the more male leaders in my church knew me, my heart, and my passions, the more they were willing to advocate for me and for my ministry. Whether formally or informally, creating connection points will build deeper relationships and allow the single person to be known by others.

For a single person who lives alone, being known by others and having meaningful conversations can be life giving. While many singles have roommates, there are a great number of singles who live alone. When a single lives alone, they naturally have no one at home with whom they are processing their day with or who is asking them how they really are. One single described the need they have for fellow staff members who will take interest in them and engage them in meaningful conversations.

> Because I spend most of my time outside of my apartment at work, if people don't ask how I am or engage in conversation with me I may go to work and be pretty stealth. I am straightforward and if someone won't stop and look me in the eye and ask me how I am, I am frustrated. I don't get to go home and have pillow talk.

Singles long for greater connections with their colleagues and may have to be intentional to seek them out. Having solid relationships with coworkers provides a huge support system for singles on staff. In a world of social media posts that give appearances that life is great, we need a place where we are fully known and cared for. It is essential that a single person on staff finds people they can talk to when they are having a bad day, who they can be with when they are feeling alone, and who are willing to ask the most important question of all—"How are you really doing?" Singles can invite their staff and colleagues to ask this question more often and in so doing build deeper connections.

Connect to Staff Families

We know that one of the greatest avenues for building healthy staff relationships is spending time together. Singles appreciate when we invite them over and incorporate them into our families. As one single shared, "A lot of my development happens in my executive pastor's home, being enfolded into their family and marital dynamic." Singles shared a wide range of experiences from being invited into the homes of other staff members to wishing they experienced more inclusion.

> My boss and his wife have two kids and they are wonderful. They would invite [me] and another single staff member over for regular dinners with their family and wanted us to know that we are a part of their family. They wanted their kids to know us and they wanted us to spend time with them and that was sweet and it was important for my development.

> My senior leader invites me over to his home. Thursday night I go to his house to watch "Survivor" with his family. There aren't scared to have me over as a single person.

> It would be nice if we could create a culture of family dinners where we were invited into each other's homes and it didn't matter if you were married or single. We shouldn't put people in a box based off marital status. I wish that would happen more on our staff.

> The moment I got engaged things changed, invitations were offered, people often welcomed us in. I received a lot more invitations to spend time together with others on staff once I was engaged. I wasn't receiving those invitations when I was single.

Another single shared how her supervisor would regularly bring his kids into the office. He wanted his kids to know the staff and wanted the staff to know his kids. He created an environment where the staff were treated like his extended family.

> My supervisor would have his kids come in and they would call us "Auntie" which is Hawaiian lingo. They considered us family because we were on staff and being single or married didn't matter.

One single shared that in her experience, families have wrongfully assumed that because she is in children's ministries and around children so much of the time, she would not want to hang out with their family. She began inviting herself and to her surprise families were shocked that she wanted to join them, yet overjoyed when she did. Some of my (Jane's) greatest memories as a single staff person was being in the home of others on our staff. Seeing them interact with their spouse and kids, feeling a part of their family, looking at the photos in their house and what is hanging on their refrigerator, these were all things that connected me to them in ways that would not happen in the office. I remember when I got engaged and one of my staff member's kids was so upset that I was getting married. They said, "You can't get married, you won't come to our house anymore, or hang out with us, or be as fun." We all laughed about it, but as I look back I really cherished those times when their family became my family. Singles need to take every opportunity to get to know other staff members families. Simple things like attending their son's or daughter's sporting events or school performances or offering to babysit for them can open the door for greater connections with staff families. Be willing to take a step toward connecting with staff families rather than waiting for them to connect with you.

Staff Gatherings

While staff get-togethers that include spouses can be challenging for singles, they are one way that we promote healthy staff relationships. I (Jane) will never forget my first Christmas season on staff at my church. I was the only single staff member at the time and we had a relatively small church staff. Our senior pastor hosted a dinner for staff and their spouses. There was no plus one in my life nor did the invitation acknowledge that I could bring anyone if I wanted to. I arrived at my senior pastor's home and certainly felt alone. It had taken a lot of courage to show up to a couples' dinner party. Everyone went out of their way to make me feel a part of it. On one hand, I was more comfortable talking to the men in the room who I worked with on a daily basis, but also felt like I was a female and should be with the women in the room who I had little to nothing in common with since most of them were stay-at-home moms. I was attempting to figure out my place in the room when the senior pastor's wife announced that we would all be moving to the table. As we arrived to the table she began assigning each couple a place across the table from one another with her and the senior pastor taking the end spots of this long rectangular dinner table. All of a sudden I realized this was like a family holiday and I was supposed to be at the kid's table, but they had managed to squeeze in one extra seat just for me. There was no one across from me, I was alone, and all I wanted to do was leave.

Unfortunately, this is how many singles feel at staff gatherings, especially if they are the only single person on staff. Singles have to put themselves out there and be willing to be uncomfortable. It can be easier for those who are on a staff with more singles, but regardless singles describe these experiences as emotionally and mentally challenging.

> I will always go and ask other single friends on staff to see if they are going [to a gathering] before I will say I will go—it is a mental preparation. It is because I am a people person, I don't care if someone is married or not, I won't feel out of place. I feel out of place a lot in my life in general, I am a young black woman that grew up in a lot of white circles, went to private schools all my life, I know how to navigate that space. But I want to be more comfortable if I can.

> Feeling alone is the biggest challenge of things. If I didn't have someone that I felt comfortable with then I would have to work at feeling comfortable so that I don't remember that I am here alone. I think that is essentially what we are trying to do to survive these spaces.

Singles have several suggestions for senior leaders as it relates to the planning of staff gatherings. These suggestions could be shared with senior leaders and make a huge difference in the experience of a single person on staff.

One suggestion might be that not all staff gatherings need to include spouses and children or for those events that do allow singles to also bring someone to the event. Interestingly enough, some singles who are dating or engaged are often made to feel that they cannot include this person until they are married. One single shared her story of being in a long-term relationship and getting engaged one week after a staff event at her church.

> There have been moments when we have bigger staff functions and spouses are invited but the person you are dating can't be. So, for me to be in a long-term relationship and we are headed towards engagement and marriage, but we are not legitimized until we are married. That is our world . . . typically though this person is a big part of our lives and they don't get to be a part of our lives completely until there is a wedding and now everyone knows this person can come to the staff functions.

Another suggestion is around how we structure Christmas dinners and other large staff gatherings. Singles can volunteer to be a part of the planning of these events so that they can speak into how the event is structured and the impact it will have on singles. They can suggest things such as open seating dinners so a single person can pick who they want to sit with, or creating more of a social stand up event where people are encouraged to mingle and there is less of a spotlight on the single person at the table who is there alone. I (Jane) know that the event I felt most comfortable at was a progressive Christmas dinner where we had four different stops at different homes and everyone mingled around the different houses. Regardless of the type of staff gathering, singles know that there are going to be moments when they are uncomfortable. It takes courage to step into large gatherings by yourself. Singles often find it helpful to be proactive and find someone on staff that they can ride with to the event and sit with once at the event. Once at the event, be willing to join in on conversations and move around in the room. All of these things will create opportunities for connecting with the broader staff community and strengthen staff relationships.

Though there are challenges as it relates to gender, marital status, and relational connection, there is much agreement that we need to create more opportunities to build healthy staff relationships. Over thirty-five times in the New Testament we see the phrase "one another." Romans 12:10, "Be devoted to one another in brotherly love," Galatians 5:13, "Serve one another," and I Thessalonians 5:11, "Build up one another," to name a few. We were created to live in community with one another. Singles long for relational connection with their leaders and fellow staff members. Building healthy staff relationships is a vital component to building a healthy church.

QUESTIONS FOR REFLECTION AND DISCUSSION

Relational connections play an important role in the well-being of staff members. The questions that follow are designed to help you think through your own relational experiences on staff and surface ideas that might help you build stronger and healthier relationships with those you work with. We would encourage you to find a close friend or colleague who you feel comfortable sharing with, as these may be good questions to discuss together.

1. How important is it for you to have relational connections with your fellow staff members? What does having healthy staff relationships look like for you?
2. Take some time to think about your own relational experiences on staff. Who is easiest for you to connect with and why? Who is most challenging for you to connect with and why?
3. In what ways does your gender impact your ability to make healthy relational connections with those of the same and opposite gender on staff?
4. How frequently do you have one-on-ones with your supervisor? In what ways could you share the importance of regular one-on-ones with your supervisor? Who else on staff would you benefit from connecting with on a regular basis?
5. How connected are you to the families of your fellow staff members? What is one thing you could do to create greater relational connection to a family on staff?
6. How often does your church do staff gatherings? In what ways would you like to see them done differently to be more inclusive for singles? How might you be involved in helping structure future staff events at your church?

Ideas for Discussion with Your Ministry Supervisor

1. In what ways do you feel connected to others on staff? In what ways do you feel disconnected from others on staff?
2. What has your experience been on our staff as a single female or male? What roadblocks have you faced because of your singleness or gender? What could we do differently to overcome these roadblocks?
3. In what ways have I or others treated you differently because of your singleness or your gender? How would you have liked for us to respond or treat you?
4. If you are a female: Single female staff members say they often feel left out, undervalued, or dismissed. Have you felt these things on our church staff? If so, when?

   If you are a male: Single male staff members say they feel cautious and careful in relating to women at church, including on staff. Have you felt that way on our church staff? If so, when?
5. How might our church staff build healthier relationships among all staff regardless of marital status or gender? Which of the suggestions for building healthy staff relationships is most important to you?

Chapter 8

Self-care and Avoiding Burnout

> *No one is going to care for you like you will care for yourself, so don't feel guilty for caring for yourself. Know what is healthy for you and what keeps you happy and healthy.*

As we have seen throughout this book, being single in ministry has both its opportunities and its challenges. One of the most resounding opportunities is the ability to serve unendlessly. Being single affords us greater freedoms to go places, to be available for ministry opportunities, and to be with people in their greatest need. But, the very thing that makes this season of life and ministry so sweet can also be the very thing that drives us to burnout.

> I have found this year more that I want to give so much because I have the time to do so, but then I become exhausted because I am not taking care of myself and allowing myself to rest, be with the Lord or be alone or engage in my friendships that I hold dear and making sure I am always investing on lateral level and instead of always pouring into other's lives.

I (Jane) remember my first year of ministry. It was filled with long days in the office, after school hangout time with kids and volunteers, and evening meetings or ministries. The weekends were times to connect with families at sporting events and a full weekend of services on Saturday and Sunday. In my first summer of ministry, I don't think I ever slept. One camp or missions trip ran into another and I was always in the midst of doing an event or getting ready for the next one. My first VBS (Vacation Bible School) I pulled an all-nighter. Yes, I said all-nighter. We were overhauling the facility after Sunday services, putting up all our decorations, getting all the details for the week assembled, when I realized it was 5:00 am. I ran home and showered so I could get back by 7:00 am for the arrival of our volunteers. A great ministry mentor once said, "Ministry is a marathon not a sprint." After that first year, I realized that if I was going to stay in ministry for the long haul I had better pace myself better. So how do we run this race with endurance when expectations seem so high?

EXPECTATIONS CAN BE HIGH

Many singles feel the added pressure to give and do more because they are single. A single person can be made to feel that they have nothing to do but ministry. Many people assume that because you are single and don't have a family at home you have more time available. The singles we spoke with were quick to point out that we all have the same amount of time in a day. As one single put it, "It is important to be in a place where people value your time even if you are single." Though singles have greater freedom around the use of their time, several expressed the sentiment that despite the expectations of others they really do want to have a life outside of ministry.

> Sometimes people can assume, especially on staff, that I should be able to do something because I don't have a family. You are freer than everyone else. But, wait, I don't want my life totally encapsulated in church, I want a life outside of church. Just because I don't have a family doesn't mean I am less than or you can take advantage of my time.

> I think we may be treated different in people thinking we are always available, everyone else who has kids and family and spouse, they are more busy or stressed, but you have nothing to be stressed about. You are single so they think you have no other responsibilities outside of work.

One female single staff member shared a story about being at a leadership retreat and the subject of having all staff work every Saturday night came up. As a student ministry leader, she already was out Tuesday, Wednesday, and Thursday nights. With great insensitivity a senior leader said, "What else are you going to do on a Saturday night?" She reflected that she was choking back tears as she felt the sense that everything in her life should revolve around church.

Somewhere along the line we have said that "family comes first" in ministry. This is certainly a true statement, but it may leave singles feeling the weight of higher expectations. Singles often hear leaders say to married staff members, "You've got kids, why don't you go home." This gives single staff persons the impression that they should always be the ones to arrive early or stay late because they are single. A single staff member can be made to feel that their time isn't as valuable as someone who is married since they don't have anyone at home waiting on them.

Conversely, singles often hear statements like, "Do you have anything going on tonight? If not, can you stay late?" Singles believe that it is all too easy to make these types of requests to singles on staff and it puts them in the position of working more than their married counterparts. In fact, some singles feel that being married creates a natural excuse to be more balanced in life and ministry. Singles don't have the married excuse and with that comes added pressure to do more and work longer hours. Several singles gave examples of how this plays out in ministry.

> I have learned I need margins, but it is a challenge because other people look at you and say, "Do you really have something to do or somewhere to go?" They may think I can stay and clean up because they need to go home to their families. We can martyr ourselves.

> At work we have a lot of special events. A lot of married people and people with kids may say, "I can't do that because my kids have a game or a practice." They have that excuse to not be there, but then they look at the single people and they say, "You don't have that excuse. So, you have to be there."

> When I was in high school ministry, we would get back from a trip and we would have to wait for students to be picked up. My colleague would say, "Is it okay if I run home and you wait with everyone because I want to see my wife and kids?" And I would say, yes. At first it was fine, but it bothered me because since I was the single one and I would work later and do more work, and in reality I had roommates that I wanted to see and I want to go home and spend time with them.

Singles are often put in awkward positions when it comes to navigating their time. On one hand, they can feel for the married staff member who hasn't seen their spouse and kids for a week. Yet on the other hand, they can feel resentment and bitterness as higher expectations are placed on them. Many expressed a willingness to go the extra mile in ministry in order to be supportive of their married counterparts, but all the while desperately wanting marrieds to value their time as much as their own. Singles often feel guilty for even thinking that wanting to get home to roommates or simply to rest is comparative to wanting to get home to a spouse or kids. Despite the tug-of-war of feelings that singles experience in these times, they have a deep desire for greater equity in work expectations. Singles find it difficult to voice this especially when it involves superiors.

> One of the most frustrating parts of ministry at my former church was that there were two of our staff that would just disappear during cleanup. We had to set up and start Sunday at 5:00 am and go to 3:00 pm with clean up afterwards, but somewhere during clean up the two married people would always disappear. It was just me and two other strong volunteers cleaning up. So instead of taking an hour it would take an hour and forty-five minutes. No one said anything. One

> guy had three kids and the other guy had no kids but they both vanished. It was unspoken and they were my superiors. How do you reprimand authority?

Greater expectations often happen around holiday services such as Christmas. There is an assumption around holidays that married people have family at home, but the single person can be at more services because they don't. Little thought may be given to the fact that even though a single staff member doesn't have a spouse or children at home, they still have families that they want to be with. I (Jane) recall my first Christmas Eve at my church. I was the Children's Pastor and we had multiple services throughout the course of Christmas Eve. At the time, I was the only single person on staff and my immediate family lived over six hours away. I booked a flight home for Christmas Day, but with weather delays I didn't arrive home for Christmas until 9:00 pm Christmas Day. Fortunately for me, when my Senior Pastor heard that I spent Christmas Day at LAX by myself, he said, "That won't ever happen again." From that day forward, I was released from being there on holidays so that I could be with my family who lived out of the area. I was fortunate to have a senior leader who responded in this way. Singles appreciate when senior leaders are sensitive to their life situations. One single shared the care that her senior pastor showed and the impact it had on her.

> Our senior pastor had asked me when I first came, it was about being with family around Christmas and he said, "You need to go be with them." The fact that he was aware of that and saying that and making that a priority and caring for me was huge. Sometimes we don't include single people like that.

Thinking through the lens of a single person can help us show greater sensitivity and care for them. While a single person can appreciate that married staff have families at home, they often wish that their time at home was valued as highly. One way to show single staff members that we value their time is to create rotations when it comes to arriving early or staying late during ministry events and programs. It isn't enough to simply ask if the single person is willing to stay late. We know they will most often say "yes" at times with much resentment. Singles long to be seen as a person with needs, cares, and concerns equally as important, even though quite different, than those who are married in ministry. One of the biggest gifts we can give a single staff member is to honor their time in the same way we honor a married person's time.

SET BOUNDARIES AND LEARN TO SAY NO

Setting boundaries and learning to say no can be difficult for all of us. In particular, since singles do have more freedom in their schedule, they often find it more challenging. They spoke also about the feeling of guilt that overcomes them when they say no to someone or something. Saying no because you need to take care of your family seems admirable. Saying no because you need to take care of yourself seems selfish. This often results in single staff members having a more difficult time creating boundaries for themselves.

I (Jane) recall that transition from singlehood to marriage at twenty-nine years of age. The first day in the office I remember thinking I actually have to coordinate my schedule with someone and commit to a time that I am going to leave the office to be home. It was both weird to think about and also a bit freeing. For the first time in my life of ministry, I had the ability to say to others, "I'll have to check our family calendar before I can commit to this." I even found others around me were more hesitant to ask me to do things because I was married. The expectation that I could and would always be available seemed to lessen. After the first month of marriage, I began to feel greater balance in my life. On top of all that, there was even someone at home who wanted to talk about more than just ministry, which was tremendously refreshing. I can see now that having a spouse actually created natural balance and boundaries in my life and ministry. Singles readily recognize that it is harder to say "no" and set boundaries without the natural accountability that comes with having a spouse.

> I don't have as much accountability around my time since I don't have a wife and family. You can be available 24/7 for students and I don't think that is healthy. I need to have boundaries and balance in my life. If you are married, you have to keep your personal and family life a priority.

> People that are married can easily say no because it doesn't work out with their spouse. I find it harder to say no because I don't have that excuse. I am single so they expect me to have the time whether it is true or not. The issue is with boundaries and realizing I am not superhuman and I don't always need to say yes because I have the time.

Even those who are "single again" and have children at home notice that it is harder to ensure boundaries for themselves and their family. One single mom shared that she felt others would respect her boundaries more if she had a spouse at home. She spoke of how it appears that others feel a sense of freedom to call her at home in the evenings because she is the only adult in the home. Several singles, but especially those with children, expressed a desire to protect their families more. Single parents return home to the job of parenting alone and share an even greater need to set better boundaries.

> If I were doing it differently, I think I would protect my energy level. Being single I am willing to give more and turn my life upside down for something to happen for someone. I probably need to have a better boundary, and my son may say I have put my ministry ahead of him sometimes.

While those married in ministry have their families to serve as boundary markers to create better balance, singles must find other ways to ensure that they create margin and space in their life for rest and renewal. The risk of not setting boundaries is burnout. It can be easy for a single person to meet with people all day and then work at home all night. A married person feels much more pressure to finish work at work so they can be fully with their family when they are at home. Singles have to be intentional about creating greater boundaries even at work. One single staff member spoke about a strategy they use at work:

> I use to keep my office door open all the time. This led to a lot of interruptions. I am a people person so I loved my interactions with people, but at the end of the day I would have to stay late or work at home to get my work done. I started telling my staff that if my door was open, come in, I am available, but if my door was closed I am working on something important so leave me alone. It sounds bad, but it really worked.

By setting simple boundaries like an open or closed office door singles can create a healthier work environment. Some shared the need to turn off their cell phone in the evening or on days off. Others talked about turning off email notifications and checking emails at set times of the day. They also affirmed how important it is to adjust your schedule after a long work day or work week.

I know myself I will give eighty hours to something, but if I do that too much, I lose sight of my boundaries and what is healthy and not healthy. I have to have boundaries in ministry because I get so passionate about the church that I can lose focus and have no boundaries.

Sometimes we can be lulled into thinking that if we don't do something it won't get done. As a pastor it can be easy to have a "savior complex," "Here I am to save the world." We know what we do is good, right, and important work. One single shared their own reflection of what has helped them most through the years:

> If I say no, the ministry will continue. This has helped me through the years. Sometimes I consult with friends who've been in ministry a long time. Also, watching pastors I work with now, seeing how they get tired, working too much, helps me understand more about myself.

SINGLES NEED VACATIONS TOO

Since singles have the freedom to work whenever and wherever, they may need greater support when it comes to taking time away from work. Ministry can encompass all hours of the day and with increased accessibility through email, texting, and social media work can become all-consuming.

In addition, some singles in ministry have to take on side jobs to supplement their incomes such as tutoring, babysitting, housesitting, or a part-time job. This can quickly lead to burnout.

> I was working on my days off doing babysitting. But, I have had to say no because I was physically getting sick because I was so tired.

> I can work anywhere, I can respond to emails anytime, work on lessons anytime. I will work a seven-hour day in the office and then work more when I get home. I can do that because I am single and home alone. It is draining when you do that because then your whole entire life is that. I love ministry, I love kids, I love all of it. It's a passion, but it is still work. So, if I am not taking time to rest I can burnout.

Some singles may feel guilty for taking time off or feel they have to justify to others why they need time off. There can be the underlying assumption that a single person "doesn't have a life" outside of ministry or that their life is a constant vacation since they don't have the same family responsibilities that a married person might have at home. Singles appreciate when the people in their life notice their hard work or long hours and encourage them to take care of themselves.

In addition to feeling guilty, it can also be challenging to plan vacations and time away since it often takes coordination with another single person's schedule. Finding others to travel with you isn't always easy. Often times, summer or holidays are typical times for vacationing; however, those are also high-intensity ministry seasons for many staff members. While others may be available to travel during those times, the person in ministry may not. Vacationing alone can only intensify the loneliness and isolation that many singles already feel, as described by this single:

> So, early on when I tried taking a mini vacation by myself, I planned on three days, but went home the second day. There were a lot of tears—a stark reminder that this is my [newly divorced] life now. I still get those moments, but less frequently.

While singles know that taking time away is an important part of self-care, it can also be painstakingly lonely if you don't have a travel partner. Several singles address this by being creative in their vacation planning. Instead of planning a trip around a specific place they want to go, they plan it around specific people they want to visit. This allows them to stay with friends along the way rather than in a hotel room by themselves and to still see some amazing sites along the way. Singles also appreciate when families on staff or in the church include them on trips. Encouraging singles to use their vacation time and helping them find creative ways to do so will affirm the need they have for rest and renewal.

FINDING SABBATH

It can be challenging for staff members to find their Sabbath, since weekends are anything but a Sabbath for those in ministry. Multiple weekend services, reviewing lessons or sermons, setting up or tearing down venues, gathering supplies, and last-minute volunteer cancellations are among several things mentioned by singles when they talk about their weekends. Singles we spoke with pointed out the need to be intentional about creating moments of Sabbath rest for themselves:

> I have had to implement a complete day of rest—my own Sabbath. It was hard in the beginning, I even didn't look at email or social media for the day. I wanted to refresh and be with God, listen to worship music. This led to me waking up early around 5:00 am to spend time reading and praying.

> I started to be more intentional about spending time with Jesus so I could minister better to the families in my church. I don't want to be an anxious soul, I want to be that calm person around everybody. If I am rushing constantly I am a hot mess and I don't have room to love others and respond to the unexpected.

> My sweet spot is at the beach or in the mountains. I often take a half day or day just to get away and be with no one but God. A lot of times I'm tempted to run errands or do laundry. Singles have those things to do to, but I know Sundays are different for me than they are for congregation members or other staff. I rarely get to go to a church service.

Finding Sabbath or a complete day of rest and removal from ministry is vital to our ability to be in ministry. I (Jane) have a few very visual memories of mentors who early on taught me my need for rest. One took an eight by ten piece of paper and asked me to write a paragraph about ministry. When I was done, he looked at me and said why did you leave this blank space around your paragraph. Without thinking I said, "Those are the margins." Puzzled that he would be questioning why my paragraph wouldn't have had margins, it dawned on me what he was implying. He gently smiled and said, "Exactly, we all need them." Another time I was working at a Christian Summer Camp and one of my leaders asked to see my calendar. Of course, at that time I actually had a paper calendar near my desk. Then he asked for a pair of scissors and began to cut out all the Friday boxes on my paper calendar. When he was done he handed me all four Fridays for the month and said, "These are yours and only yours. You can do with them as you want, but guard these days with your life because what you do with these days will determine how far you are able to go in ministry." It was a simple concept, but one that left an indelible mark on me. Symbolically my mentors were giving me permission to rest and to take time for myself in the midst of so many demands on my time and attention.

Creating space for ourselves also creates space for others. In the busyness of our lives, we can find ourselves having less capacity for others. We may miss opportunities to connect with people that are important to us. We may miss out on important conversations with people around us. In our calendared lives, there is no room for the unexpected to occur. Singles we interviewed spoke of the need to create space for rest, renewal, and refueling of their mind, heart, and spirit on a regular basis:

> There is no margin for the unexpected to happen so I need to make room in my mind, heart and spirit for the unexpected. Like making margin for friends who call with a need so I can be there. But, if I was in such a hurry and didn't take time to be with the Lord I would be frustrated and miss out on these moments.

> I haven't perfected this, but a perfect example today I was so tired and I slept through all my alarms and I woke up at 8:30 and was supposed to be in at 9:00 and my day started later. I still spent fifteen minutes with the Lord, praying and reading [the] Word, doing devotional, and then while I was getting ready for work and had worship music on. Having that on was so calming for me.

INVEST IN YOURSELF

While it's always important to take time to invest in yourself, singlehood may afford more time and space to do so. The need for continued physical, mental, emotional, and spiritual growth is evident for everyone in ministry. Those in ministry may find that their spirituality becomes professionalized. Pastors must guard against the tendency to allow the doing of ministry to become a substitute for cultivating our own relationship with Christ. It can be easy to have sermon and lesson preparation replace our own time in the Word, or a prayer meeting replace our own time talking with Jesus. Even though ministry leaders are directing others spiritually, they also need spiritual direction themselves. As one single stated, "It is helpful to process things with my spiritual director and to have a huge reminder that I am just a follower of Jesus. Christianity is not my job."

Though singlehood is a season of life that allows a person to be more focused on themselves, singles are often so focused on ministry to others that they don't take the time to invest in themselves. The singles we interviewed were quick to point out that one of the best things a single person can do is take time to work on themselves and build greater relational connections with others. The following are a list of ideas that singles found helpful as they reflected on investing in themselves during their season of singlehood:

- Grow in your emotional and spiritual health—work on yourself, meet up with mentors, therapists, spiritual directors, and counselors. Do the hard work of digging into wounds of the past that might cause issues in the future. Find people who can challenge you spiritually and help you be a better leader.
- Participate in a young adult ministry at another church where you can be "you" and not "a pastor on staff."
- Find people willing to commit to pray with and for you. Have people in your life who you can call any time day or night and they will pray for you.
- Take up a new hobby. Learn something new. Challenge yourself to do things you never thought you could do.
- Seek healthier habits to release the stress of ministry in a positive way—go on a walk, get a gym membership, choose to eat better, or cook at home.
- Make new friends. Get involved in a peer group in a church or in your local community where you can engage in going out, having fun, and embrace new experiences with a group of like-minded people.
- Pursue an advanced degree to broaden your own base of knowledge.
- Read from a wide array of disciplines (theology, practical ministry, leadership, business, etc.). Take advantage of the time to read, study, and learn as much as you can.

FINDING SUPPORT

When it comes to self-care and avoiding burnout, singles welcome greater support from those around them. It can be all too easy for those in ministry to focus on giving and helping others grow to the detriment of their own growth. Singles are greatly encouraged when someone in their life cares enough to look out for them and check in on them, especially in regard to their spiritual health and well-being. They appreciate the person that is willing to simply ask, "How are you doing," and then really listen. Singles appreciate those who encourage them to live well-rounded lives by taking time off, getting rest, and attending to their spiritual lives. In many ways, this affirms their own desires for greater work life balance and gives singles permission to do so. Singles may have to be intentional about creating a support team around them. A few singles shared ideas that have been helpful to them.

> Find someone you can be completely honest with. Bad things happen in the dark. Singles are often going it alone and there are a lot of temptations out there. You need people who can shine light in your life. Be wise in who you select to

be that person. It can be someone on the church staff or in the congregation, but more common and safer might be someone outside the church.

> Reach out to others when you are struggling. Have people to process things with—a combination of friends from outside the church and those inside the church. I have people outside to engage with who bring a healthy more objective perspective. They can share their perspective based on how they know me—it centers me.

Singles also find it helpful when leaders in the church create informal or formal connection points. One of the challenges of singleness is relational isolation. There isn't necessarily anyone in particular that is checking in with you or on you. Some singles have immediate family members that call and check in, but often they can miss the daily interaction and life accountability that comes with having a spouse. In those times, having pastors and elders who make a point to touch base, check in, and provide support toward healthy self-care is a welcomed encouragement.

> My pastor and I are on separate floors, we don't see each other, but sometimes when he is leaving he will check in and say hello and if I am there late [which I do a lot] he will say you need to go home. I appreciate that even though I don't always listen, but he is trying to look out for me and guard me.

> There is a gal who is an elder, probably a little younger than me, and has some young kids and she serves in my ministry. She is willing to help and pray and is super supportive—always checking in on me. She will stop by my office and say hi and ask how she can pray for me or she will text me just to check in.

It can seem at times that leaders are more concerned about those who are married on staff than those who are single. Since there is a lot of emphasis on the health of a pastor's family and their marriage, it can feel to a single person that their health isn't as important. One example of this might be a pastor who sees a marriage conference coming up and encourages the guy on staff to attend it with his wife or a congregation member that offers their vacation home to a couple on staff so they can get away. Though these things are important for the health and vitality of those married in ministry, singles appreciate when leaders in the church also look out for and advocate for them.

> I would appreciate a leader not waiting for a single person to ask for permission for time off, but go to them and say, "You had a long summer and why don't you go away for a weekend?" Pursuing singles and saying, "I have this idea for you because I want you to take care of yourself" and not waiting for us to ask for permission. It would be nice if they valued our health as much as they value those who are married on staff.

In addition to having individuals in your life who provide accountability, support, and encouragement, many singles expressed how meaningful it is to be a part of a mixed life group with marrieds and singles. Though singles may find it difficult to find a mixed group to be a part of, they appreciate when they do. Singles notice that in mixed groups the focus shifts away from dating and toward spiritual growth and community, which they long for. They enjoy interacting with married people who often have different perspectives on life. They are encouraged by opportunities to be a part of a married person's family. They express the benefit it can be to see a Christian marriage being modeled before them.

We have a great opportunity before us to support singles on their ministry journey. Whether leveling the expectations placed on singles, helping them to set and keep boundaries that will sustain their ministries, or encouraging them to find rest and renewal along the way, singles long for greater support around them.

QUESTIONS FOR REFLECTION AND DISCUSSION

Avoiding burnout and being in ministry for the long haul is something we all desire. In order to do so, we know that we have to be intentional in caring for ourselves. The questions that follow are designed to help you think through your own experiences and surface ideas that might help you better care for yourself. We would encourage you to find a close friend or colleague who you feel comfortable sharing with, as these may be good questions to discuss together.

1. What unwritten expectations have others placed on you because of your singleness? How have you dealt with these expectations?
2. On a scale of 1–5 (1 = my tank is empty, 3 = my tank is half-full, 5 = my tank is full), how would you rate your health and well-being? If you find yourself a 1, 2, or 3, what do you need to do to fill up your tank?
3. What boundaries have you set for yourself in ministry? What boundaries would be helpful for you to establish for yourself? In what ways would these boundaries benefit you and others?
4. Do you regularly disengage from ministry during your days off? If not, what do you need to do to make your days off more restful for you?
5. What types of activities replenish your soul? How can you create more opportunities for these in your life?
6. How do you find Sabbath rest in the midst of a busy ministry schedule? What is one thing you could do this next week to create a Sabbath for yourself?

7. How might you use this season of your life and ministry to invest more in yourself? What is something you would love to pursue? If you were able to do this, what would it bring to your life and ministry? What would you have to change to do this?
8. Who is your biggest support in ministry? What support do you need to seek out for yourself?

Ideas for Discussion with Your Ministry Supervisor

1. In what ways might our staff and church place higher expectations on single staff members than on those who are married? What can we do to change this?
2. How can our leadership team better support your health and well-being in ministry?
3. How might our church encourage your spiritual growth as a single person?
4. What can supervisors do to help singles establish better ministry boundaries and create margin for rest and renewal?

Appendix 1

Open Letter to Church Leaders

Please feel free to copy and use this letter to help communicate with your ministry team. We ask that you simply include the credit line: This letter is taken from the book, Thriving as a Single Person in Ministry *(Lawson, K. and Carr, J., 2021. Rowman & Littlefield.)*

Dear Church Leaders,

As a single person on staff at your church I wanted to take a moment to write to you. While I know that you were once single too, your experience may not have been my experience and perhaps it has even been a while since you were single. I experience many joys and challenges when it comes to being a single staff person. I thought it might be helpful if I shared a few of them with you.

One of the greatest joys I experience is such freedom to serve however, whenever, and wherever I want. I love that I can go on mission trips, hang out with students on a Friday night, flex my schedule to help others, and show up early and leave late at ministry events. When I am at a church event or camp I feel like I can be fully present. My interests aren't divided between my family and my ministry and that gives me such singularity of focus. This season of life allows me time and space to deepen my relationship with God and others, be more generous with my time and money, and invest in my own growth and development. There is so much to celebrate about this season of my life.

While there are many joys and opportunities in being single, there are also many challenges that I face. I don't think these challenges are always seen by others and that is why I am writing to you. Honestly, sometimes it is really hard to be on staff as a single person. So much of the church is structured around families, the events we offer, the programs we do, the sermons and illustrations we give. I often feel like an outsider. I face daily social expectations to be married and sometimes I feel like everyone around me thinks something is wrong with me. I think some in the church have forgotten that Jesus and Paul were single, and about I Corinthians 7 where Paul speaks about the advantages of being single—being free from concern, not having divided interests, having an undivided devotion to the Lord. I wish that we talked about this more in the church so that people saw the good aspects of my singleness.

I must admit that there is a part of me that wants to be married, but I don't always want to be "set up" by others and dating can be challenging in the fishbowl of ministry where everyone's eyes are on me and the person I date. I know I don't always show it, but sometimes I face financial struggles as a single. I can't afford to live on my own and find myself having to rent a room or have multiple roommates. That isn't always easy. I often feel like I have to work two jobs or find side work to help support myself. That leaves me tired and worn out. Perhaps the pay is also related to promotability as well. I know some churches won't hire me for certain positions and certainly others make me feel like I have to be married to ever do more than what I am doing now.

Before I close there are just a few more things I want to share. Even though you might not see it on the outside, I often feel the pains of loneliness on the inside. This can be especially true when there are so few of us who are single on staff. Staff Christmas parties and events where spouses and families are invited are often painful reminders to me that I am alone. Sundays are often the worst day of the week for feeling lonely. Families fill the church and even in a crowd of people I am aware that I am alone. Sometimes a week can go by and I realize that I haven't really had a deep genuine conversation with anyone in my life.

I know you are probably wondering at this point in the letter, "What can I do to help?" You have done so many things that have helped me through these challenges. I have appreciated the times you have asked me how I am doing and taken the time to help me process through things. I love it when you take time to meet with me individually and invite me into your home and family life, when you anticipate what I might need as a single person and value me for who I am. It means so much to me when you are planning an event or preparing for a sermon and you ask me, "How will this impact a single person in our church?" It helps when you notice that I'm working too much and tell me to go home or encourage me to take time off. I appreciate when you see me as a person more than you see my singleness.

Thank you for picking up this book. I think it is all too easy for people to assume that they know how single staff are doing or what they need, but

I would encourage you to take the time to talk with them and ask them. In fact, at the end of each chapter there are great questions to discuss with the singles on your staff like me.

Thank you for supporting me on my journey!

A Staff Member (who happens to be single)

Appendix 2

Resources for Singles in Ministry

The limited published material in this field is reflected in what we have been able to find on the topic to date. Special thanks to Santa Rusliana and Joo Chang Jang, my research assistants over the past few years, for their help in finding these items to aid our research. We trust that these may also be helpful to those who want to read more on this topic, whether for their own benefit or to help in supervising and supporting others. (Kevin E. Lawson)

BOOKS, CHAPTERS, AND THESES/DISSERTATIONS

Armstrong, R. 2005. "For Pastors Who Are Single." In *Help! I'm a Pastor: A Guide to Parish Ministry*, 54–57. Louisville, KY: Westminster John Knox Press.

Barton, R. J. 1991. *Sex in the Parish*. Louisville, KY: Westminster/John Knox Press.

DeRosia, M. L. 2011. *The Girlfriends' Clergy Companion: Surviving and Thriving in Ministry*. Herndon, VA: Alban.

Hawker, D., and T. Herbert. 2013. *Single Mission: Thriving as a Single Person in Cross-Cultural Ministry*. Condeopress.com (e-book).

Masters, A., and S. Smith. 2011. "Romancing the Reverend: Singleness, Sex, Divorce, and Dating." In *Bless Her Heart: Life as a Young Clergy Woman*, 33–44. St. Louis, MO: Chalice Press.

Ratcliffe, C. E. L. 2017. "All the Single Ladies, All the Single Ladies: Young Clergywomen's Experiences." Master's Thesis. Atlantic School of Theology, Halifax, Nova Scotia. http://library2.smu.ca/bitstream/handle/01/27046/Ratcliffe_Caitlin_GRP_2017.pdf?sequence=1&isAllowed=y.

Rediger, G. Lloyd. 1986. *Single Pastors*. New York: Episcopal Church Center.

Zikmund, B. B., A. T. Lummis, and P. M. Y. Chang. 1998. "Single Clergy." In *Clergy Women: An Uphill Calling*, 34–37. Louisville, KY: Westminster John Knox Press.

JOURNAL ARTICLES

Britton, S., and K. Rapp. "Called to Be Single: Issues and Concerns of Single Women in Ministry." *Lutheran Education* 142, no. 2 (2008): 87–95. http://search.ebscohost.com.ezproxy.biola.edu/login.aspx?direct=true&db=eue&AN=508034799&site=eds-live.

Chang, P. M. Y., and P. Perl. "Enforcing Family Values? The Effects of Marital Status on Clergy Earnings." *Sociology of Religion* 60, no. 4 (1999): 403–417. http://search.ebscohost.com.ezproxy.biola.edu/login.aspx?direct=true&db=aph&AN=2714592&site=eds-live.

Crawford, C. A. "Ministry from a Single Perspective: Assets and Liabilities." *The Journal of Pastoral Care* 42, no. 2 (1988): 117–123.

Jordheim, A. "A Sympathetic Look at the Lifestyles of Unmarried Clergy." *Lutheran Forum* 13, no. 1 (1979): 8–10. http://ezproxy.biola.edu/login?url=http://search.ebscohost.com/login.aspx?direct=true&db=rfh&AN=ATLAiB8W170613000297&site=ehost-liv.

Kness, L. A. "Confessions of a Single Pastor." *The Christian Ministry* 17, no. 1 (1986): 8–10.

Lin, Y., C. Li, B. Irby, and G. Brown. "Exploring Taiwanese Female Pastors' Intimate Relationships: Using the Story of the Levite's Concubine." *Counseling & Values* 58, no. 2 (2013): 142–157. https://doi.org/10.1002/j.2161-007X.2013.00030.x.

Nesbitt, P. D. "Marriage, Parenthood, and the Ministry: Differential Effects of Marriage and Family on Male and Female Clergy Careers." *Sociology of Religion* 56, no. 4 (1995): 397–415. http://search.ebscohost.com.ezproxy.biola.edu/login.aspx?direct=true&db=asx&AN=9512290933&site=eds-live.

Richmond, L. J. "Stress and Single Clergy Women." *Psychotherapy in Private Practice* 8, no. 4 (2008): 119–125. DOI: 10.1300/J294v08n04_12.

Richmond, L. J., C. Rayburn, and L. Rogers. "Clergymen, Clergywomen, and Their Spouses: Stress in Professional Religious Families." *Journal of Career Development* 12, no. 1 (1985): 81–86. http://ezproxy.biola.edu/login?url=http://search.ebscohost.com/login.aspx?direct=truedb=psyh&AN=1986-29844-001&site=ehost-live.

Swenson, D. (1998). "Religious Differences between Married and Celibate Clergy: Does Celibacy Make a Difference?" *Sociology of Religion* 59, no. 1 (1998): 37–43. http://www.jstor.org/stable/3711964.

Williams, S. "Single. Female. Pastor." *Mutuality* 21, no. 3 (2014): 12–14. http://ezproxy.biola.edu/login?url=http://search.ebscohost.com/login.aspx?direct=true&db=aph&AN=98723092&login.asp&site=ehost-live.

POPULAR ARTICLES, ONLINE ARTICLES, NEWSPAPER ARTICLES, BLOGS, AND THE LIKE

Allberry, S. "Where Are All the Single Pastors?" *Crossway Articles* (blog), February 27, 2019. https://www.crossway.org/articles/where-are-all-the-single-pastors/.

Almlie, M. "Are We Afraid of Single Pastors?: If Being Unmarried Was Good Enough for Jesus and Paul . . ." *Christianity Today* (blog), January 31, 2011. https://www.christianitytoday.com/pastors/2011/january-online-only/are-we-afraid-of-single-pastors.html.

Almlie, M. "Are We Afraid of Single Pastors? (Part 2): Where Did the Prejudice against Single Pastors Come from, and How Do We Move Past It?" *Christianity Today* (blog), February 2011. https://www.christianitytoday.com/pastors/2011/february-online-only/are-we-afraid-of-single-pastors-part-2.html.

Atchison, D. C. "All the Single Lady Preachers." *Young Clergy Women International* (blog), January 11, 2011. https://youngclergywomen.org/all-the-single-lady-preachers/.

Beal, A. "Frustrations of Being Single in Ministry." *Young Church Leaders* (blog), January 3, 2017. http://youngchurchleaders.org/2017/01/03/frustrations-single-ministry-redeem/.

Briggs, D. 1997. "Single Clergy: Unattached Pastors Face Challenges in Building Intimate Relationships." *The Spokesman-Review*, August 16, 1997. http://www.spokesman.com/stories/1997/aug/16/single-clergy-unattached-pastors-face-challenges/.

Campbell, H. "Ten Truths about Dating as a Single Woman in Ministry." *The Youth Cartel* (blog), December 11, 2014. https://theyouthcartel.com/ten-truths-dating-single-woman-ministry/.

Carroll, C. "Single White Female Pastor." *The V3 Church Planting Movement* (blog), March 6, 2017. http://thev3movement.org/2017/03/single-white-female-pastor/.

Conner, K. "The Double-Edged Sword of Singleness in Youth Ministry." *Rooted Ministry* (blog), June 26, 2017. https://www.rootedministry.com/blog/double-edged-sword-singleness-youth-ministry/.

Daniel, B. "Single Pastors, Biblical Counseling, and the Local Church." *9Marks Journal* (blog), March 20, 2017. https://www.9marks.org/article/single-pastors-biblical-counseling-and-the-local-church/.

Davis, K. "Finding a Place for Single Pastors." *Think Christian* (blog), April 8, 2011. https://thinkchristian.reframemedia.com/finding-a-place-for-single-pastors.

DeWitt, S. "Single vs. Married Pastors: Take It from a Guy Who's Been Both." *The Gospel Coalition* (blog), March 13, 2014. https://www.thegospelcoalition.org/article/single-vs-married-pastors-take-it-from-a-guy-whos-done-both-2/.

Driscoll, M. "Mark Driscoll: Single Pastors?" *Ministry Today Magazine*, January 9, 2014. https://ministrytodaymag.com/leadership/personal-character/20636-mark-driscoll-single-pastors.

Eckholm, E. 2011. "Unmarried Pastor, Seeking a Job, Sees Bias." *The New York Times*, March 21, 2011. https://www.nytimes.com/2011/03/22/us/22pastor.html. (Originally a version was published in the New York edition, Section A, Page 1, "With Few Jobs, a Single Pastor Points to a Bias.")

Highfill, L. "Ten Things Every Single Woman in Ministry Wants You to Know about Her." *Hope for Pastor's Wives: A Sanctuary for Weary Hearts website* (blog), February 17, 2014. http://embracingrace.com/2014/02/ten-things-single-women-ministry-wish-understood/.

Hodson, K. L. "Going It Alone: The Challenges and Joys of Being Single in Ministry." *The North American Division of Seventh-Day Adventists. NAD Ministerial* (blog), February 11, 2018. http://www.nadministerial.com/stories/2018/2/4/going-it-alone-the-challenges-and-joys-of-being-single-in-ministry.

Jackson, A. "Why We Need Single Women Leaders: The Unique Challenges and Powerful Insights of Unmarried Ministry Leaders." *Christianity Today. Womenleaders.com* (blog), September 21, 2017. http://www.christianitytoday.com/women-leaders/2017/september/why-we-need-single-women-leaders.html?paging=off.

Lathrop, J. "Are Singles as Qualified for Ministry as Married People?" *Charisma Leader* (blog), September 9, 2014. https://ministrytodaymag.com/life/singles/21199-are-singles-as-qualified-for-ministry-as-married-people.

Lawless, C. "10 Reflections of a Formerly Single Pastor." *Church Leaders* (blog), December 13, 2017. https://churchleaders.com/pastors/pastor-articles/315031-10-reflections-formerly-single-pastor.html

Lee, D. J. "Confessions of a Single, Female Pastor." *Marie Claire* 18, no. 2 (February, 2011): 87.

McKeever, J. "What Churches Should Know When Their Pastors Are Single." *Charisma Leader* (blog), September 5, 2018. https://ministrytodaymag.com/life/relationships/25350-what-churches-should-know-when-their-pastors-are-single.

Mohler, R. A. "Must a Pastor Be Married? *The New York Times* Asks the Question." *Albert Mohler* (blog), March 25, 2011. https://albertmohler.com/2011/03/25/must-a-pastor-be-married-the-new-york-times-asks-the-question.

Okwu, C. C. "Pastoring While Single: The Challenge and Beauty of Navigating Small-Group Ministry Alone." *Christianity Today. SmallGroups.com* (blog), June 1, 2016. https://www.smallgroups.com/articles/2016/pastoring-while-single.html?paging=off.

Russell, K. "Single at 28 (and 82)." *Young Clergy Women International Magazine* (blog), October 3, 2017. https://youngclergywomen.org/single-28-82/.

Schaeffer, A. "Why My Singleness Matters." *CL Chuck Lawless* (blog), September 13, 2018. http://chucklawless.com/2018/09/why-my-singleness-matters/.

Schilling, C. "The Single Pastor." *The Presbyterian Outlook* (blog), December 30, 2014. https://pres-outlook.org/2014/12/single-pastor/.

Stevens, N. "Challenges of Being a Single Leader in Ministry." *Single Matters* (blog), 2015. http://www.singlematters.com/challenges-of-being-a-single-leader-in-ministry/#.

Taber, D. "Why God Loves Single Pastors (And Your Church Should Too!)." *Viral Believer*, May 1, 2017. https://www.viralbeliever.com/bible-studies/single-pastors/.

Vanderaa, S. "Going It Alone: Being Single in Youth Ministry." *Youth Specialties* (blog), 2017. http://youthspecialties.com/blog/going-alone-single-youth-ministry/.

Walter, D. "The Single Minister: One in Christ." *Christian Standard*, March 3, 1996: 8–9.

Appendix 3

Background on the Single Church Staff Study

Once we decided to pursue this writing project, there were three phases to our research effort. First, we conducted a literature review of both research and popular writing on issues related to vocational ministry in the church when single. We located only one research publication. The remainder came from a wide range of chapters in books, magazine articles, and blogs, representing a mix of personal experiences and broader observations on challenges singles face in vocational ministry in the church. Most of these materials appear in appendix 2 in the resources list.

After reviewing the existing literature, we summarized what we learned and developed the two primary areas of focus for our own research efforts. First, we wanted to better understand the opportunities and joys of vocational ministry when single and how to maximize them. Second, we also wanted to better understand the challenges of vocational ministry when single and how to manage them well. Our hope was that, together, these lines of inquiry would lead to a better understanding of both how singles in ministry could thrive and how to help others thrive. This led to a phenomenological research approach, seeking to understand the lived experience of a particular group of people, in this case, single church staff members.

In the second phase of the study, we recruited single church staff members to participate in focus groups to explore their experiences and see what kinds of opportunities and joys they identified in their ministries, what challenges they experienced, and what they did to address those challenges. We recruited people through two main efforts, involving both convenient and snowball samplings. First, Kevin connected with Mick Boersma, a colleague who works with seminary alumni from Talbot School of Theology, a nondenominational school with alumni serving in a wide range of denominational settings, church sizes and locations, and representing diverse ethnic groups.

Mick combed through their large database to identify single church staff members to consider for the planned focus groups and interviews. We invited all of those Mick identified, and most agreed to participate. Second, Jane has served on church staff in Southern California for well over twenty-five years and has been involved in several church staff networking organizations. In addition, she has also taught in the undergraduate ministry leadership programs for over twenty-five years and knows most of the alumni from these programs. Jane reviewed information on graduates and ministry leaders on the West Coast of the United States and identified whom to invite to participate in the study. Again, most agreed to do so.

Kevin led two focus groups of single men, and Jane led two groups of single women. This was done to encourage more open sharing within each group, as they may have felt awkward discussing some issues with people of the other gender present. These focus groups were very helpful for surfacing issues and learning how common they were, but we found being in a group could hinder open sharing on more sensitive topics. We recorded the sessions and analyzed the data that came from these group conversations, compared what we heard from the men and the women, and then identified major themes that we wanted to explore further through personal interviews.

In the third and final phase of the research, we carried out individual interviews with single church staff members, seeking a wide diversity related to age, denomination, and ministry roles. These interviews, which ranged from forty-five minutes to well over an hour, took place in different locations, including restaurants, offices, on the phone, and online using WebEx or Zoom. We again explored the opportunities and joys of ministry, as well as the range of challenges they experienced, and we followed up to explore their thinking more deeply and the experiences behind what they shared. We continued the interviews until we were not hearing any new perspectives, issues, or themes (theoretical saturation). We completed a total of thirty-nine interviews, twenty men and nineteen women. All told, with the focus group participants, we heard from forty-five single church staff members in our focus groups and interviews. Table A.3.1 is an overview of the demographic data about who participated in our focus groups and interviews.

As we carried out the interviews, we reviewed the recordings, taking extensive notes and making transcripts of portions or entire interviews.[1] We met together to develop and discuss a master list of themes and subthemes that emerged from the interviews and focus groups. Then we reviewed these themes and identified clusters of subthemes on different topics, resulting in the chapter structure of this book.

We took care to consider the wide range of experience of the different participants in the research, not just topics voiced by a majority of those interviewed. While most were Caucasians in their twenties and thirties who

Table A.3.1 Demographic Data on Focus Group and Interview Participants

Demographic Variable		*N*
Gender:	Male	20*
	Female	25**
Age:	Range	22–73
	20s	20
	30s	9
	40s	8
	50s	5
	60s	1
	70s	1
Ethnicity:	Caucasian	33
	Korean American	4
	African American	2
	Hispanic American	2
	Chinese American	2
	Filipino-American	1
	Immigrant (Nigeria)	1
Marital Status:	Never married	33
	Recently married	4***
	Divorced	4
	Widowed	2
	Engaged	1
	Separated	1
Years in Ministry While Single:	Range	<1 to 47 years
Church Attendance:	Range	25–8,000+
	Under 100	2
	100–500	9
	501–1,000	13
	>1,000	21
Denominations:	Anglican Church in North America	
	Assemblies of God	
	Baptist	
	Christian Church	
	Evangelical Free Church	
	Evangelical Lutheran Church of America	
	Evangelical Presbyterian	
	Free Methodist	
	Independent Christian Church	

(*Continued*)

Table A.3.1 Continued

Demographic Variable		*N*
	Lutheran	
	Nondenominational	
	North American Christian Church	
	Parachurch Youth Ministry (2)	
	Quaker–Friends Church	
	Reformed Presbyterian	
Staff Roles:	Administration/Operations	
	Associate Pastor	
	Children's Ministry	
	Creative Arts Ministries	
	Disabilities Ministries	
	Family and Student Ministry	
	Lay Person Preaching Team	
	Missions and College Ministry	
	Recovery Groups Ministry	
	Senior/Solo Pastor	
	Small Groups/Connections Ministry	
	Student/Youth Ministry	
	Worship	
	Young Adult Ministry	

Notes:

* Each of the seven men who participated in focus groups was also interviewed.

** Nineteen of the twenty-five women were interviewed, including three who had been in focus groups.

*** These four were recently married and had at least a few years of ministry experience while single and also after being married. This allowed a unique opportunity to explore changes in their experience.

were never married, we also wanted to represent well the experiences of older staff members, those who were widowed or divorced, single parents, solo and senior pastors, various associate staff members, and people serving in various ethnic minority and immigrant church contexts. While there is a great diversity of ministry roles, ages, ethnicities, and denominational groups represented in the study, the sample has a high percentage of people serving in larger church contexts, mainly in Southern California, with a stronger representation of evangelical congregational settings than mainline church contexts.

We encourage others to build on this research, going even deeper in exploring different themes, including church staff from other denominations, other regions of the United States, more diverse community types (rural, small town), and sizes of congregations. We can still learn much more that can help those who serve in vocational ministry while single to thrive.

Notes

INTRODUCTION

1. Kevin E. Lawson, *How to Thrive in Associate Staff Ministry* (Herndon, VA: Alban Institute, 2000).

2. Kevin E. Lawson and Mick Boersma, *Associate Staff Ministry: Thriving Personally, Professionally, Relationally* (Lanham, MD: Rowman & Littlefield, 2014); Kevin E. Lawson and Mick Boersma, *Supervising and Supporting Ministry Staff: A Guide to Thriving Together* (Lanham, MD: Rowman & Littlefield, 2017).

3. If you are interested, you can read more about the research project behind this book in Appendix 3.

4. See https://www.census.gov/content/dam/Census/library/visualizations/time-series/demo/families-and-households/ms-2.pdf.

5. See https://www.census.gov/content/dam/Census/newsroom/facts-for-features/2017/cb17-ff16.pdf.

6. See https://www.cnn.com/2018/01/05/health/single-people-partner/index.html.

7. Two recent books on a theology of singleness that are worth reading and considering include C. S. Hitchcock, *The Significance of Singleness: A Theological Vision for the Future of the Church* (Grand Rapids, MI: Baker Academic, 2018) and J. M. Bennett, *Singleness and the Church: A New Theology of the Single Life* (Oxford, UK: Oxford University Press, 2017).

8. Special thanks to my colleague, Dr. Mark Saucy, professor and co-chair of the Department of Theology at Talbot School of Theology, Biola University, for meeting with me and reviewing my initial draft of this material. Conversation is a great way to learn, and his input strengthened this section.

9. For a helpful discussion of these issues, see J. Hellerman, *When the Church Was a Family: Recapturing Jesus' Vision for Authentic Christian Community* (Nashville, TN: B&H Academic, 2009).

CHAPTER 4

1. Single female children's ministry director in her forties reflecting on her financial challenges.

CHAPTER 5

1. A male staff member with four years' ministry experience while single, and four years' experience since being married, reflecting on the job application process.

CHAPTER 8

1. For the men's interviews, we took detailed notes from the recordings, and made transcripts of comments relevant to various identified themes. For the women's interviews, we made full transcripts, and then focused on different sections for more detailed analysis.

Index

About the Authors

Kevin E. Lawson serves as Professor of Educational Studies in PhD and EdD programs at Talbot School of Theology, Biola University. He served as a church associate staff member for eleven years before moving to seminary teaching, and his research continues to focus on the needs of associate staff members. He is the coauthor of *Associate Staff Ministry: Thriving Personally, Professionally,* and *Relationally and Supervising and Supporting Ministry Staff.*

Jane Carr serves as Professor of Christian Ministries at Talbot School of Theology, Biola University. She served for twenty-six years at a large church in Southern California where she was involved in children's ministry, student ministry, singles' ministry, church administration, and staff training and development. She has conducted seminars, workshops, and teacher trainings both nationally and internationally. She is the founder of Focus on Leaders providing executive leadership coaching and leadership training to ministry leaders and business executives. She is certified in the Gallup Strength Finder, the Leadership Circle Profile, the Emotional and Social Competency Inventory, and the Myers-Briggs Type Inventory.

Made in the USA
Middletown, DE
16 November 2021